TECH IN THE TRENCHES

Strategic Inventions of the Civil War

Ann Byers

Cavendish Square

New York

Published in 2016 by Cavendish Square Publishing, LLC
243 5th Avenue, Suite 136, New York, NY 10016

First Edition

Website: cavendishsq.com

CPSIA Compliance Information: Batch #CW16CSQ

All websites were available and accurate when this book was sent to press.

Cataloging-in-Publication Data

Names: Byers, Ann.
Title: Strategic inventions of the Civil War / Ann Byers.
Description: New York : Cavendish Square Publishing, [2016]
| Series: Tech in the trenches | Includes index.
Identifiers: ISBN 9781502610300 (library bound) | ISBN 9781502610317 (ebook)
Subjects: LCSH: United States — History — Civil War, 1861-1865 — Juvenile literature.
| United States — History — Civil War, 1861–1865 — Technology — Juvenile literature. |
Technology — United States — History — 19th century — Juvenile literature.
Classification: LCC E468.9 B94 2016 | DDC 973.7'301—dc23

Editorial Director: David McNamara
Editor: Kristen Susienka
Copy Editor: Nathan Heidelberger
Art Director: Jeffrey Talbot
Designer: Alan Sliwinski/Amy Greenan
Senior Production Manager: Jennifer Ryder-Talbot
Production Editor: Renni Johnson
Photo Research: J8 Media

The photographs in this book are used by permission and through the courtesy of: Ortodox/Shutterstock.com, cover; Buyenlarge/Getty Images, 4, 28, 34–35, 45, 71; Ann Ronan Pictures/Print Collector/Getty Images, 9; North Wind Picture Archives, 12, 23; Library of Congress, 14; John Wollwerth/Shutterstock.com, 26; Public Domain/File:Battle of Guiliford Courthouse 15 March 1781.jpg/Wikimedia Commons, 39; Public Domain/Dept. of the Navy/File:Blockade-runner2 ADvance.jpg/Wikimedia Commons, 40; MPI/Getty Images, 42; Underwood Archives/Getty Images, 48; Library of Congress, 50, 83; Patrick Guenette/Alamy Stock Vector, 54; Steve Estvanik/Shutterstock.com, 60; Public Domain/Winslow Homer/File:The surgeon at work at the rear during an engagement (Boston Public Library).jpg/Wikimedia Commons, 62; The Print Collector/Print Collector/Getty Images, 64; Universal History Archive/UIG/Bridgeman Images, 74; Public Domain/Yale University Libraries/File:East and West Shaking hands at the laying of last rail Union Pacific Railroad - Restoration.jpg/Wikimedia Commons, 79; National Archives/File:Confederate torpedo boat David aground at Charleston, South Carolina, 1865 - NARA - 533129.tif/Wikimedia Commons, 85; Chronicle/Alamy Stock Photo, 88; Das48/File:ACELA Express.JPG/Wikimedia Commons, 92; Oleksiy Mark/Shutterstock.com, 94; Puttawat Santiyothin/Shutterstock.com, 97; U.S. Navy photo courtesy of General Dynamics, 100.

Printed in the United States of America

CONTENTS

INTRODUCTION 5
The War That Changed America

ONE 15
Antebellum America

TWO 29
Preindustrial War

THREE 43
The First Railroad War

FOUR 55
Barrels and Bullets

FIVE 65
Wood and Iron

SIX 75
After the War

SEVEN 89
Civil War Technology Today

GLOSSARY 103

BIBLIOGRAPHY 105

FURTHER INFORMATION 108

INDEX 109

ABOUT THE AUTHOR 112

Members of the New York Eighth Militia, a volunteer regiment. Thirty-eight soldiers in the militia were killed, wounded, or captured at Bull Run, the first major battle of the Civil War.

INTRODUCTION

The War That Changed America

The first half of the nineteenth century was an exciting time for the United States. The six decades between 1800 and 1860 were years of explosive territorial growth, phenomenal technological innovation, rapid economic transformation, and unprecedented social reform. They were years of prosperity and progress; thousands of foreigners came to America to share in its promise.

However, it was also a time of deepening division. An imaginary line drawn from east to west roughly across the middle of the United States would separate the country into two distinct regions: North and South. These two sections, faced with the same forces of change, developed very differently during this time. Their economic, social, and political courses took entirely different directions. The gulf between them grew steadily wider and more contentious until it erupted in the bloodiest conflict in American history. This era is known as the **antebellum** period because these were the years before the Civil War (*ante* means "before" and *bellum* means "war").

EXPANSION

Between 1800 and 1860, the United States more than tripled in size. Through purchases, wars, treaties, and shrewd negotiations, the country expanded from 865,000 square miles (2.2 million square kilometers) to almost 3 million square miles (7.8 million sq km). In 1800, the western border of the new nation was the Mississippi River, although most Americans lived on a fairly narrow swath of land along the Atlantic Ocean. Three years later, the purchase of the Louisiana Territory from France pushed the western boundary to the Rocky Mountains. After war with Mexico and a foray into Texas in the 1840s, the country stretched all the way to the Pacific. An agreement with Great Britain added the vast Oregon Territory.

This was the beginning of **manifest destiny**, the idea that the geography and the ideals of the United States could and should extend from "sea to shining sea." Taking the values of liberty and rugged individualism from coast to coast was considered the obvious (that is, manifest) destiny of a people so enlightened and so blessed. In the antebellum period, the number of states grew from sixteen to thirty-three.

The country also increased in number of people. Natural growth plus immigration swelled the population from 5.3 million in 1800 to six times that number, 31.4 million, in 1860.

ECONOMY

At the beginning of the nineteenth century, the overwhelming majority of Americans were farmers. Everything they produced, from their crops to their clothing and their houses, was made with human or animal power. That changed dramatically after Samuel Slater brought the Industrial Revolution from England to the United States. That event, as its name implies, revolutionized industry; work once performed by muscle could now be performed by machines. Items handmade at home could be mass-produced in factories.

In America, the Industrial Revolution progressed from a single cotton-spinning mill in 1791 to hundreds of textile factories in the 1820s to more than 140,000 manufacturers in 1860. The industries churned out all sorts of products from nails to railroad cars. The US display at the first world's fair, London's 1851 World Exhibition, showcased many American inventions. Europeans were amazed by such technological wonders as Cyrus McCormick's mechanical reaper, Charles Goodyear's vulcanized rubber, a Day and Newell lock that could not be picked, and Samuel Colt's repeating revolver.

All these items were made in the North. The transition from agriculture to industry took place largely in the North, where rocky soil and harsh weather made farming difficult. In the South, fertile fields and a mild climate were ideal for producing tobacco, rice, cotton, sugar, and other crops easily. Nevertheless, the South might have turned from farming to factories also were it not for Eli Whitney's invention of the cotton gin.

Prior to the introduction of the machine in 1794, cotton was not a particularly valuable crop. Separating cottonseeds from the plant's fibers was too time consuming to be worth what the cotton would sell for. The gin, however, made the process fifty times faster. Demand for cotton was high, so growing cotton became very lucrative. US cotton production jumped from 750,000 bales in 1830 to 2.85 million bales in 1850. All over the South, landowners tore out their other crops and replaced them with cotton. Those who had money bought more land and planted more cotton. Cotton became "king," and the South was firmly committed to maintaining its agricultural economy.

SOCIETY

The two different economic bases created two different societies. In the North, the shift from producing goods by hand to using machinery lured people from their scattered farms to centrally located factories. The move began with mill towns that housed and employed young women. Before long, thousands of men and women flocked to where the jobs were. By 1860, less than half the working population of the country was still engaged in agriculture. Rural villages and small towns had been replaced by cities of tens of thousands.

The self-acting spinning mule required very little human help to turn cotton into thread. The child under the spindles at the left was paid to sweep up lint.

The large urban centers housed a variety of people enjoying new opportunities: business owners, merchants, bankers, shippers, and factory workers. Job openings attracted immigrants from Europe. The wage labor system of the factories created a middle class. The Northern cities had an egalitarian society—that is, all citizens had the same rights.

In the South, most of the farms were small or medium sized. A very small number of Southerners—about a quarter of the entire population—owned large farms, or plantations. However, that quarter possessed most of the money in the region and all the power. They were the ones with enough property to be able to vote and hold political office. (Some states did not remove property qualifications until as late as 1856.) Their wealth and political prestige placed them far above everyone else on the social pyramid. The social structure of the antebellum South was an aristocracy—a small minority at the top and the large majority beneath them.

At the very bottom of the social ladder were four million slaves (in 1860). Before widespread use of the cotton gin, slavery in America had been slowly but steadily declining. For many, the cost of keeping slaves had been more than the profit slaves brought. In the North, slavery had already been completely abandoned; by 1804 all the Northern states had abolished the practice. But once cotton plantations became thriving commercial businesses, slavery became an essential element of the region's economy.

TRANSPORTATION

Many in the North tolerated the South's slavery for economic reasons. The agricultural economy of the South and the industrializing economy of the North fed each other. The textile mills in the North turned the cotton from the South into cloth, and the planters in the South bought the North's manufactured goods. Both regions shipped some of their goods to markets in the West and in other countries.

This new economy—a market economy based on supply and demand—required new and better forms of transportation. The supply of raw materials and finished products had to be moved to where the demands were. Thus the Industrial Revolution sparked a transportation revolution.

Transportation networks were needed that crossed the Appalachians and connected the different parts of the country. In the early 1800s, a series of toll roads were built, almost all in the North. The owners erected gates every five or ten miles and placed poles with pikes, or spikes, across the gates. When travelers paid the toll, the pikes were turned aside to allow the travelers through the gate. Hence the toll roads were called "turnpikes." In addition, the federal government built the 800-mile-long (1,287-kilometer-long) Cumberland Road, or National Road, to facilitate trade between Cumberland, Maryland, and Vandalia, Illinois.

The roads sped the transport of goods, but waterways were even faster. For years people dreamed of connecting the lakes in the Midwest with the rivers of the East, and even the ports on the Atlantic. That dream was realized in 1825 when the Erie Canal linked the Great Lakes with the Hudson River. The 350-mile (563 km) canal dramatically reduced the cost of shipping, opened up new areas of the country, increased commerce between regions, and created a new transportation industry. It also ignited a flurry of canal building. By 1840, more than 3,000 miles (4,828 km) of canals spanned waterways from New York City to New Orleans.

However, these innovations paled in comparison with what replaced them. The steam locomotive was one of the most impactful innovations of the Industrial Revolution. It slashed shipping costs and cut a day-long trip to less than an hour.

Trains could carry the heaviest and bulkiest cargos up steep mountains. Between 1830 and 1860, railroad companies laid over 30,000 miles (48,280 km) of track across the United States.

SOCIAL REFORM

The profound changes of this period had some negative consequences in the cities of the North. Working conditions in the factories were sometimes difficult and dangerous. Abandoning farms had put some into debt. The concentration of people in cities bred crime.

Early canal boats were pulled by horses or mules or powered by steam. This artist's depiction of the Erie Canal in the 1800s shows horses on a towpath pulling a barge.

The prosperity and the urban lifestyle gave people, particularly women, the time and means to address these issues. Many were likely motivated by preachers of the Second Great Awakening, a religious revival that swept the entire country at the beginning of the century. Others, with the War of Independence still in their memories, may have simply wanted to see the promise of "life, liberty, and the pursuit of happiness" extended to all Americans. Whatever the reasons, numerous social reform movements sprang up. People joined societies and mounted crusades dedicated to such varied causes as caring for orphans, the blind, and the mentally ill; improving conditions in workplaces and in prisons; establishing public education for children; granting rights to women; and outlawing alcohol (called the temperance movement).

Some of the reformers were concerned about matters beyond their own cities. Many wanted to see the slaves of the South receive their freedom and the practice of slavery abolished. **Abolitionists**—people who were actively involved in this effort—may have intended to bridge the divide between North and South, but they actually deepened it. It would take a four-year war before the gap would start to close. The American Civil War was about all the issues in the sectional divide—political as well as economic. Fought in the midst of the Industrial Revolution, it pioneered several new technologies born of that revolution. After the Civil War, battlefield communication, troop transport, and weaponry would be never be the same.

Senator Henry Clay of Kentucky argues for the Compromise of 1850.

CHAPTER ONE

Antebellum America

At the beginning of the antebellum period, most Americans were somewhat comfortable with the country's sectional division. One reason was that the two sections needed each other. The South bought manufactured goods from industrialists in the North. The North depended on the Southern plantations for the cotton that kept its textile mills in operation.

The majority did not make an issue of slavery, a major factor in the division. They accepted the reasoning of South Carolina senator John C. Calhoun, who called slavery "the peculiar institution of the South." Calhoun explained that slavery was permitted only in the South and the Southern states depended on it for their very existence. He was right; slavery was peculiar to the South and without it the economy and social order of the Southern states would collapse.

Most people in the North, even those who abhorred slavery, thought the practice would eventually fade out on its own. They saw it gradually wane in the border states of the upper South. As long as slavery was confined to the South, mostly the **Deep South**, they were content to leave it alone to die a slow death.

POLITICAL BATTLEGROUND: THE WEST

However, the plantation owners could not confine slavery to the South. Cotton, as profitable as it was, ruined their fields. Planting the same crop year after year took nutrients out of the soil. The landowners' solution was not to plant different crops or industrialize; it was to acquire new land. Plenty of farmland had become available after the Louisiana Purchase in 1803. The new territory would be divided and organized into states. The planters needed to purchase some of that property, and they needed to be allowed to take their slaves into that territory.

Many Northerners were dead set against permitting slavery in the West. They were as determined to create **Free States**—states where slavery was illegal—in the western territory as the Southerners were to establish slave states. Their motives were mixed. Some were abolitionists who believed slavery was immoral and should be eradicated from the entire country. Others had political reasons.

The political battle was not about slavery but about power. In addition to slavery, the North and the South had different, sometimes competing, economic interests. For example, tariffs on foreign imports protected Northern manufacturing but harmed Southern exports. Federal spending on roads often benefited one region more than the other. These and other matters that divided North and South were debated and settled in Congress. As long as the two sides were equally represented in Congress, power was balanced fairly evenly. But if one side had more representatives and senators, that section would win all the political contests. Every Free State added to the **Union** gave the North more congressmen and thus more power; every slave state gave the South an advantage.

At first, admissions of new states seesawed between free and slave states: Ohio was admitted as free, then Louisiana as slave; Indiana as free, then Mississippi as slave; Illinois as free, and Alabama as slave. For about twenty years the country functioned in relative peace with an equal number of Free States and slave states. The first major challenge to that fragile balance came when residents of the Missouri Territory petitioned Congress for admission to the Union as a slave state.

Despite the fact that the Missourians asked for admission as a slave state, some Congressmen tried to ban slavery in the new state. Heated arguments raged in Congress for a year. The matter was finally resolved in 1820: Maine was carved out of Massachusetts and admitted as a Free State and Missouri was

Eli Whitney Begins and Ends the Civil War

Eli Whitney is best known for his invention of the cotton gin. Because that invention made slavery extremely profitable, he is sometimes said to have started the Civil War. He is less known for developing—or, more accurately, promoting—a process that probably contributed to ending the war.

The cotton gin made Whitney famous but did not bring him much money. Looking for some income, he accepted a contract from the US War Department in 1798 to manufacture ten thousand muskets. Failing to deliver the weapons on time, he explained that he was designing machinery that would produce better weapons more quickly. At that time, guns were made by hand, one at a time, by skilled craftsmen. It was a long and expensive process.

Whitney proposed using interchangeable parts. Laborers rather than craftsmen would make the separate parts of the guns by machine and assemble multiple weapons in a short time. He demonstrated to skeptics at the War Department by bringing a supply of parts and constructing muskets in front of them. They extended his contract and he delivered the weapons—eight years late.

Eli Whitney did not come up with the idea of using interchangeable parts, which he called "uniformity," but he did popularize it. It became known as the American system of manufacturing. The forerunner of the assembly line, it enabled industrialists to use less-skilled, lower-paid workers. Because the North had the factories and the process, uniformity helped the Union to mass produce more weapons and thus win the Civil War.

accepted as a slave state. The solution was known as the Missouri Compromise. The balance of power was maintained at twelve Free States and twelve slave states.

THE ISSUE: A UNION OR A CONFEDERACY?

Although the compromise calmed the immediate crisis, it raised a larger question: Did the federal government have the right to make rules for the states? The compromise included stipulations concerning parts of the Louisiana Purchase territory that were not yet states. It prohibited slavery north of a line that ran along the southern border of Missouri and extended westward. Southerners asked how the federal government could outlaw slavery for a state before the people of the state even formed a government. Who was in charge of the affairs of a state—residents of the state or members of Congress?

At this early stage of the nation's history, Americans did not have a strong sense of national identity. Many thought of themselves as citizens of their states more than as citizens of the country. They considered the United States a confederation of separate states joined together by compact, or agreement. Because the states created the federal government, they were above it. This position, called states' rights, was held by most Southern politicians by the end of the antebellum period.

Many other Americans held a different position, called federalism. They believed that once the states ratified the Constitution, the United States became a union, a single entity rather than a collection of states acting independently. States had rights over local issues, but the federal government set the rules for national matters. If federal and state ideas clashed, the federal idea prevailed. Northern politicians generally held this position.

The debate over states' rights versus federal rights often revolved around slavery, but it also was part of other controversies that separated North from South. The issue was raised again and again in the years leading up to the Civil War. It was the question answered on the battlefield. The essence of the issue was whether the United States was and would be a confederation of separate states or an indivisible union.

THE ISSUE IN CONGRESS

The issue first surfaced in a major way in 1828 when Congress imposed a high tax on imports. Southerners called the tax the "Tariff of Abominations." It helped Northern manufacturers, but it hurt Southerners, who wanted to buy the imported goods at low prices. South Carolinians decided they would not honor the tariff. They declared the law null and void in their state. They threatened to **secede** from the Union if Congress tried to collect the tax.

President Andrew Jackson could not let the nullification of a federal law stand. He prepared to send an army to South Carolina to enforce the tariff there. Instead, the situation was defused. Henry Clay, the Great Compromiser who came up with the Missouri Compromise, led Congress in rewriting the tariff law in 1833. The new law reduced the tax enough to convince South

Carolinians to withdraw their nullification decree. The crisis was averted … for the moment.

The issue would appear again when new land was acquired in the West. Would that land be slave or free? In 1846, as President James Polk sought money to fund the negotiation of a treaty ending the Mexican War (which had only just begun), Representative David Wilmot suggested that no slavery should be allowed in any territory gained in the treaty. This was called the Wilmot Proviso. Because of the North-South balance in the Senate, however, the Wilmot Proviso failed. The argument was quieted.

The quiet held until Congress received California's application for statehood … as a Free State. Without a slave-state application for balance, tempers flared. The months-long dispute finally ended when Henry Clay proposed five laws that together came to be known as the Compromise of 1850. The compromise did not settle the underlying issue, but it had something for both sides. Among other items, the North got California admitted as a Free State and the South got a promise that the residents of the Utah and New Mexico Territories could decide the issue of slavery for themselves. The South also got a concession that upset Northerners: the Fugitive Slave Act. The law required that if a slave escaped to a Free State, the people in that state had to return the slave to his or her owner. Despite that law, the compromise eased tensions a little … but only for a very short time.

Four years later, western land was again the focus of controversy. Illinois senator Stephen Douglas wanted to see

Nebraska become a state so a railroad could go through Nebraska and connect Illinois with cities on the Pacific coast. But Nebraska was north of the Missouri Compromise line; it would be a Free State. The only way Douglas could get Southerners to approve his proposal was to give them a slave state. He suggested Kansas, but Kansas was also north of the 1820 line. Congress would have to repeal the Missouri Compromise.

That is exactly what happened. The Kansas-Nebraska Act allowed the formation of two new states, erased the Missouri Compromise line, and allowed the residents of the new states to decide whether they would be slave or free. The action did not ease tensions; it kindled them into violence.

BLOODSHED

The decision was to be made by "popular sovereignty." That is, the people who lived in the territory would vote on whether the state would be free or slave. No one doubted that Nebraska would be a Free State. Nebraska was fairly far north and not suited for growing cotton. Stephen Douglas fully expected Kansas to become a slave state. It shared a border and climate with the slave state of Missouri.

Douglas had not counted on the strong emotions and dogged determination of so many people on both sides of the issue. Nebraska went as expected, but Kansas became an actual battleground, with guns and swords. Abolitionists and others in the North sent thousands of settlers into the area so they would outnumber the proslavery residents when time came for the election. At the same time, thousands of proslavery activists

This illustration shows abolitionist John Brown seizing the federal arsenal at Harper's Ferry, Virginia, in 1859. He was hoping to start a slave uprising, but instead he was captured by US Marines under Colonel Robert E. Lee.

from Missouri crossed into Kansas to intimidate and harass the free-state settlers and stuff the ballot box. Dozens of skirmishes, raids, and assaults led to about fifty-five deaths. Horace Greeley, publisher of the *New York Tribune,* called the seven-year struggle "Bleeding Kansas." When it was finally over, Kansas emerged as a Free State.

THE ELECTION OF 1860

By 1860 the North-South rift was so wide the political parties could no longer span it. The Democratic Party split into Northern and Southern wings. The Whig Party completely dissolved and was replaced by a new Republican Party made up entirely of Northerners. A number of concerns confronted the nation in 1860—tariffs, immigration policy, a transcontinental railroad, and homesteading—but the overriding political issue was the matter of slavery in the Western territories. The Southern Democrats' position was that the right to hold slaves should be protected in the territories. The Republicans were against the expansion of slavery. The Northern Democrats tried to please both sides. They supported popular sovereignty, assuming the territories would become Free States.

The Republican nominee for president in 1860 was Abraham Lincoln. Lincoln's stand on the all-consuming topic of slavery was clear: slavery was immoral but lawful. It should be allowed to remain where it was but should not be permitted to expand to new states. Lincoln's position on states' rights was also plain. Two years previously he had declared, "A house divided against itself cannot stand. I believe this government cannot endure permanently half slave and half free … It will become all one thing or all the other."

Southerners believed that if Lincoln were elected the "one thing" the "house"—the United States—would eventually become was all free. They could not let that happen. But their party was divided. The Northern and Southern wings each put up its own candidate. To make matters worse, a fourth party put yet another name on the ballot. When all the votes were counted, Abraham Lincoln had only 40 percent of the popular vote but enough electoral votes to win. He had carried all the Free States and not a single slave state.

SECESSION

Two days later, South Carolina declared Lincoln's election a "hostile act" that forced the state to secede, or withdraw, from the United States. Within six weeks, on December 20, South Carolina had issued a formal Ordinance of Secession. It solemnly declared that "the union heretofore existing between this State and the other States of North America, is dissolved, and that the State of South Carolina has resumed her position among the nations of the world, as a separate and independent State."

To the secessionists, the action was the logical and only end of the states' rights argument. They saw revoking their compact with the Union as a second War for Independence, on a par with the Revolutionary War. In fact, they modeled their Ordinance of Secession after the Declaration of Independence. The *Charleston Mercury* newspaper likened the actions of its state to those of earlier Patriots: "The tea has been thrown overboard, the revolution of 1860 has been initiated."

Within weeks of South Carolina's declaration, the six other states of the Deep South followed suit. Before Lincoln even took office, the seven states had joined together as the Confederate

States of America and elected Jefferson Davis as president. Outgoing president James Buchanan did little to quell the revolt.

Lincoln tried. In his inaugural address he assured an angry South that he had no intention "to interfere with the institution of slavery in the States where it exists." He promised that he would enforce the Fugitive Slave Act. But the main issue in the sectional divide was no longer slavery. It was states' rights; specifically, the right of individual states to leave the Union. On that issue Lincoln

Fort Sumter, seen here, was built on a sandbar reinforced with granite after the War of 1812 to guard the entrance to Charleston Harbor.

would not budge. In the same speech, he insisted that the United States was not "an association of States" but a perpetual Union. That meant, he warned, that "no State upon its own mere motion can lawfully get out of the Union; that *resolves* and *ordinances* to that effect are legally void."

WAR

The new president's appeals fell on deaf ears. The states of the Confederacy had already begun seizing federal property within their borders. One of the most important of those properties was in Charleston, South Carolina, the largest city in the South. Several forts guarded the entrance to the harbor. Within days of seceding, state troops easily took possession of all but the largest, Fort Sumter.

On April 11, 1861, barely a month after Lincoln took office, South Carolina brigadier general P. G. T. Beauregard demanded that federal soldiers surrender Fort Sumter. When the demand was refused, Beauregard ordered one of his cannons fired at the fort. Thirty-four hours later, the fort was surrendered and the Civil War had begun.

Part of the drum corps of the New York Eighth Militia. Many of the sixty thousand musicians of the Civil War were men too old and boys too young to fight.

CHAPTER TWO

Preindustrial War

The Civil War has been called the first industrial war, at least the first in America. It was waged with technologies birthed in the Industrial Revolution, and the victor was the one who had the edge in those technologies. All the essential elements of warfare—communications, transportation of troops and supplies, and weaponry—were different from those of the past because of the innovations of industry. To understand the tremendous impact of the new technologies on the Civil War, it is helpful to look at the ways Americans fought before the Industrial Revolution.

COMMUNICATION

In the 1700s and early 1800s, military commanders communicated in much the same way they had for centuries.

Officers' orders could not be heard over great distances, especially in the din of battle, so musical instruments were used to signify specific action. Infantries—foot soldiers—used bagpipes, drums, and fifes. Cavalry soldiers could not play these instruments on horseback, so they used whistles, bugles, and other types of horns.

The drummers and fife players of the Revolutionary War were a primary link between the commanders and the soldiers. Their tunes told men when to march, whether to turn right or left, when to load their weapons, and when to fire them. When a battle ended, the musicians played "Cease Fire" and soldiers at the edges of the field knew they could relax. If an officer wanted to talk with the enemy's commander under a flag of truce, he directed the musicians to play "Parlay." Everyone knew the tunes that signaled attack and retreat. The drummer and fife player would begin, and drum and fife teams some distance away would pick up the song. In camp, the music of the drum and fife or the bugle woke the soldiers in the morning and told them when to retire for the night. Different tunes signaled times for meals, times for various chores, and times to gather. During marches, the music set the pace and kept spirits up.

Musical instruments and barked commands generally worked well for communication between officers and soldiers on the battlefield, but what about communication between commanders about larger concerns of **strategy**? What happened, for example, when a general fighting in one area needed an officer in another location to send reinforcements? Or if an officer wanted to issue new directions to different regiments? For strategic communication—the overall coordinating and directing of operations—officers used the communication methods employed from ancient times: face-to-face meetings and sending messages.

These methods had drawbacks. For one, they were dangerous. Lone figures in a war zone aroused suspicion as well as gunfire. Stonewall Jackson was fatally shot by his own sentries when he returned from a nighttime meeting with his officers. For another, couriers could be intercepted. Benedict Arnold's treason was uncovered when a letter was found in a courier's boot.

In addition to the danger, messages carried by foot, on horseback, or by boat could take a long time to reach their destination. In the War of 1812, a single exchange of information between the War Department in Washington, DC, and Andrew Jackson commanding forces at New Orleans required six weeks. Even after steamboats replaced river barges, communication was slow. During the Mexican War in 1847, a message from Zachary Taylor in Texas took three weeks to reach Washington.

Thus, preindustrial tactical communication—directing the activity on the battlefield—was fairly effective. However, strategic communication—coordinating among officers the details of when and where the battles would be fought—was woefully inadequate. Fortunately for those fighting the Civil War, a technological innovation of the industrial age revolutionized communication between war departments and commanders on the field. The telegraph, first used in 1844, could provide almost real-time

Wig Wag

One means of tactical communication pioneered in the Civil War was developed by army surgeon Albert Myer. When the doctor was in medical school, working as a telegraph operator, he created a communication system for the deaf based on the two elements of the telegraph signal. As an army major, he figured out how to adapt the system for use on a battlefield. The result was wig wag, a flag-waving form of communication, and the birth of the Army Signal Corps.

The code was simple. Starting with the flag above the signaler's head, a wave to the left was "1," a wave to the right was "2." As in Morse code, every letter could be represented by some combination of these two numbers. For clarification, a wave directly in front of the signaler was a "3"; one, two, or three 3s would indicate the end of a word, sentence, or message.

Signalmen waved their messages from high ground, on specially built signal platforms, or sometimes strapped to trees. The flags could be seen for 15 miles (24 km) on a clear day. At night, the flags were replaced with kerosene torches.

In refining the wig-wag system, Myer was assisted by a young lieutenant from Georgia. When war began, the assistant resigned from the Union Army and began a signal corps for the Confederacy. Both North and South then had to encode their signals. Wig wag proved useful. By the end of the war, the US Signal Corps numbered about 300 officers and 2,500 men.

communication. But for the telegraph to work in military settings, there first had to be significant improvements in transportation.

MOVING THE MILITARY

Military transportation involves more than moving soldiers. When General George McClellan invaded Virginia in 1861, he brought men, animals, and 700 tons (635 metric tons) of food for each day. He also transported field artillery, ammunition, tools for building fortifications, tents and bedding, and other materials. Prior to the Civil War, only two modes of moving equipment and supplies were possible: wagons and boats.

The bulk of an army's travel was over land, where it had to rely on very slow horse- or mule-drawn wagons. Over the best roads, columns of wagons could travel only 10 to 12 miles (16 to 19 km) a day. Harsh weather, poor roads, and rugged or steep terrain slowed them further. Broken axles stopped them altogether. If an opposing army destroyed a bridge, the carts carrying cannons and supplies were stranded until it could be repaired. In 1781, when George Washington moved the Continental Army from what is now Greenburg, New York, to Yorktown, Virginia, his men had to repair roads, rebuild river boats, and find food for their animals. The 500-mile (805 km) trek took six weeks.

Large armies required many wagons, and the long supply trains were vulnerable to attack. A train of one hundred wagons stretched over a mile of road, making it a very big and very attractive target. When Winfield Scott invaded Mexico in 1847, he had to assign more than one thousand soldiers to guard his supply train from bands of guerrillas.

The Fifth New Hampshire Infantry built this bridge across the Chickahominy River in two days so a large army could reach a battle site. It was called the Grapevine Bridge because the logs were lashed together with grapevines.

The deficiencies of preindustrial transportation would be overcome with the advent of the railroad. Steam-powered trains could cover great distances over rough terrain in all kinds of weather. They could carry large amounts of heavy loads in covered cars safe from attack—and they could do it in record time. Safe, reliable, rapid military transportation was available through railroads. All that was necessary was to apply the technology to the battlefield.

FIREARMS

Preindustrial weaponry was also deficient. It was slow and not very accurate. The standard weapon of the infantry soldier of the Revolutionary War was the musket. A musket is a light gun, weighing about 9 pounds (4 kilograms), fired from the shoulder. The stock and barrel together gave it a length of about 60 inches (152 centimeters). A 15-inch (38 cm) knife blade, called a bayonet, was attached to the muzzle if hand-to-hand combat was expected.

Muskets were loaded from the muzzle, the end of the barrel where the shot exits the weapon. The entire process of shooting

Pratt Street Riot

The first blood of the Civil War was spilled at a railway station in a fight over transportation. After Fort Sumter was fired upon on April 12, 1861, President Lincoln called for seventy-five thousand men to come to Washington to quell the rebellion and defend the capital. The Sixth Massachusetts Militia responded. The soldiers traveled by rail from Boston to Baltimore, where they had to change trains. The two trains were owned by two different companies and the stations were ten blocks apart. A local ordinance prohibited steam locomotives in the city, so rail cars were pulled between stations by horses.

It was a simple train transfer, but the air was tense. Like many other places at the onset of the war, Maryland in general and Baltimore in particular was torn between Union supporters and Southern sympathizers. The soldiers rode in their horse-drawn cars down Pratt Street, but a mob of Southern sympathizers blocked their path. The soldiers had no choice but to walk the remaining eight blocks. As they marched, people determined to keep them from the train hurled bricks and stones at them. A shot rang out and frightened soldiers fired back. The protest escalated into a full-scale riot. Police finally managed to stop the violence and escort the soldiers to the train station, but not before four soldiers and twelve civilians were killed and twenty-four soldiers and an unknown number of civilians wounded. After the Pratt Street Riot, Southern sympathizers in Maryland destroyed rail lines in an attempt to prevent any more Union forces from traveling through their state.

the weapon, from inserting the powder to positioning and firing, required nine to twelve steps. A well-trained soldier could fire no more than four shots per minute. But the shots did not necessarily hit their targets. Muskets were typically smoothbore firearms. That is, the **bore**—the inside of the barrel—was smooth. The "bullets," which were actually lead balls, were smaller than the diameter (**caliber**) of the barrel. The barrel of the typical musket was .75 caliber and the standard lead ball was .69 caliber. The ball had to be smaller than the barrel because every time the musket was fired, soot from the powder clung to the inside of the barrel, narrowing the barrel's diameter. The difference in size meant the ball banged against the barrel as it sped toward the muzzle, slowing it down and keeping it from going straight. The maximum range for a musket was 100 yards (91 meters).

Because of the weapon's short range and poor accuracy, musketeers did not actually aim at specific targets. They fired in volleys. The soldiers stood shoulder to shoulder in lines two or three rows deep. At the command to fire, the men in the first row knelt and raised their weapons. This enabled those in the row or rows behind them to position the long barrels of their muskets over the shoulders of their comrades. Everyone fired at once in the general direction of the enemy. If the armies were close enough, some balls were bound to hit someone.

The musket was not the only weapon around at the time. Hunters preferred the rifle, a shoulder firearm with longer range and greater accuracy. Early rifles were essentially muskets with rifled barrels. **Rifling** is a pattern of spiral grooves cut along the inside of the weapon's barrel. The grooves keep the lead ball from hitting the sides of the barrel and instead make it spin. This allows the ball to go straighter, farther, and with greater force. With a nineteenth-century rifle, a good marksman could hit a target at a distance of 400 yards (366 m), four times farther than with a musket. But rifles were problematic in battle. Because the ball fit more tightly than in a musket, it took longer to load. The tighter fit also meant the soot buildup had to be cleaned more often. Also, repeatedly ramming the ball down the barrel damaged the rifling. Thus, despite the rifle's advantages, the musket remained the army's common infantry weapon into the Civil War.

The officers, who often directed the fighting from horseback, and the cavalry could not use shoulder-fired weapons; they had pistols. Like muskets, the pistols were smoothbore, muzzle-loaded, single-shot weapons.

The type of firearms an army possesses dictates the **tactics** of battle. Leading up to the Civil War, the approach to fighting was to wear down and overwhelm the enemy one step at a time. The first step was the volley. The idea was to send a hail of lead balls into the opposing lines with the hope the enemy would scatter, retreat, or fall. If the volley was not sufficient, the next step was a bayonet charge. The goal was the same: kill, wound, or chase the foes. Once the opposing lines were thinned and weakened, the cavalry came in to finish the job.

A number of developments shortly before and during the Civil War improved the accuracy and effectiveness of weapons. Weapons that were loaded from the breech, or rear, rather than the muzzle removed the shortcomings of rifles. **Repeaters**—rifles that could fire several shots before needing to be reloaded—had obvious advantages over single-shot weapons. The most significant

In this painting of the Revolutionary War Battle of Guilford Courthouse, you can see British soldiers in volley position at far right, colonials beginning a bayonet charge, and the cavalry sweeping in.

The *Advance*, a steam and sailing ship, was a Confederate blockade runner that got through the Union blockade of North Carolina ports at least twenty times before being captured by the Union.

improvement was the invention of the minié ball, a completely new and utterly devastating type of bullet. This bullet, together with the new weaponry that used it, radically altered the tactics of war.

WAR ON THE SEAS

Technological improvements of the industrial age also affected naval warfare. The preindustrial warship was a wooden vessel powered by wind. It was basically little more than a platform for soldiers and cannons. Its wooden construction left it vulnerable to explosive shells. Its dependence on wind limited its maneuverability. The space taken up by the masts and rigging gave it too little room for soldiers. Sailing ships were fine for coastal transportation, but they were clumsy in war.

Nevertheless, warships were absolutely necessary in the Civil War. One of Lincoln's first decisions at the outbreak of war was to blockade Confederate ports. The South depended on imports and desperately needed to keep its ports open. In order to defend more than 3,000 miles (4,828 km) of coastline, Southern leaders were forced to figure out how to upgrade their preindustrial navy. Thus the South was at the forefront of the major naval technological innovations.

Steamships had already begun to replace sailing vessels. They were smaller, faster, and easier to maneuver, making them excellent blockade runners. Out of the need to protect the ships that were vital to securing the ports came more innovations: iron sides, underwater mines, torpedoes, and even submarines.

The nation went into the Civil War as an industrializing society. Many of the tools and methods it had for fighting had been used for decades, but its generals had new technologies that could be brought to the battlefield. Its leaders had factories that could produce them. Many aspects of military communication, transportation, and weaponry first used in the American Civil War shaped armies and navies for generations thereafter.

Both Union and Confederate troops used railway guns, often surplus naval cannons mounted on flatcars.

CHAPTER THREE

The First Railroad War

In addition to the labels of "first modern war" and "first industrial war," the American Civil War has been called the "first railroad war." Steam-powered trains were still relatively new when the war broke out; the first railroad company in the United States began service in 1826. By 1861, 30,000 miles (48,280 km) of track already wound through the country.

That track did more than carry merchandise and people: it carried messages. The communication technology of the Industrial Revolution, the telegraph, grew with the railroad. Early railroads often had just one line of track between stations for both incoming and outgoing trains. To avoid collisions and to schedule runs, conductors needed to communicate between stations. Railroad companies were happy to let telegraph companies string wires on their land along their rail lines and place their telegraph offices in or near the rail stations. Thus the railroad radically improved communication as well as transportation.

Until 1861, both the telegraph and the railroad had been used only for peaceful purposes. The Civil War was the first major conflict to exploit these technologies. In war, a railroad is a **logistics** tool. Logistics is the science of providing support for military operations. It involves getting, storing, and transporting people, equipment, and supplies. It is the aspect of military operation that puts the resources required for an engagement in the place they need to be. In the Civil War, railroads replaced horse- or mule-drawn wagons as a means of transporting materials to theaters of operation.

An often-quoted military saying is: "Amateurs study tactics; professionals study logistics." In other words, the most important consideration in any military operation is not what to do on the battlefield, but how to get the right personnel and materials to the conflict. The most brilliant battle plan will not succeed if the supplies to execute it do not reach the field. Logistics is often more critical than tactics in determining victory. In the Civil War, the railroad was a revolutionary logistics technology used by both sides. If the saying is accurate, whichever side had the better railroads was bound to win the war.

NORTHERN SUPERIORITY

The North had obvious advantages over the South in regard to railroads. Two-thirds of the nation's track—21,000 miles

The locomotive *John C. Robinson* during the siege of Petersburg

(33,796 km)—were located in Union territory; the Confederacy had only 9,000 miles (14,484 km). This might not seem such a great disparity, considering that the South had only 40 percent of the country's population, but the track in the North was much more practical. The railroad lines of the South were short and disconnected; they had been built to carry agricultural products from isolated areas to ocean and river ports. In the North, where raw materials and manufactured goods were constantly exchanged, nearly all cities were interconnected through a vast rail network.

In both regions, the tracks had been laid by scores of companies working independently. The lines of the different companies did not connect; even in the same cities, the station of one rail line was generally a mile or more from the station of another. Goods traveling long distances would have to be offloaded from one train, transported to another, and reloaded. To make matters more difficult, at the beginning of the railroad-building boom, different companies used different gauges. That is, the space between the rails of one company's tracks was not the same as the space of another company's. More than twenty different gauges could be found, making it impossible for trains to travel on any track except their own. Companies in the North recognized the benefits of connecting, and they began early to adopt a uniform measure. By 1860, most of the railroads of the North operated on a standard gauge. In the South, however, cotton growers had little need to link their lines, so the use of different gauges persisted.

The North's industrial base gave it another advantage. Even before the war, nearly all the manufacturing facilities producing materials for building, repairing, and replacing railroad track and equipment were located in the North. The South had never had the ability to maintain its railroads on its own. It had very few factories that could produce quality rails, much less engines or cars. It imported nearly all its rails from England or bought them from the North. Soon after the war began, the South converted any factories that could make railroad engines and parts to armaments production. Supplies from the North stopped completely and a Union blockade kept out materials from England.

SOUTHERN SUCCESSES

Although the North had more and better railroads, the South made greater use of the technology in the first two years of the war. That is largely because the bulk of the war was waged in the South. Even though the Southern railroads were disjointed, the fact that the Confederate generals fought where they had access to their railroads gave them tremendous advantages.

Southern generals were quick to grasp the value of the railroad for the movement of supplies to combat locations. Before long, the railroad's usefulness in troop transport also became evident. In the opening battle of the war, called First Manassas by the Confederates and First Bull Run by the Union, the South owed its victory to the railroad. The Union plan was to put a stop to the rebellion by capturing Richmond, the Confederate capital. In July 1861, a Union army of thirty-five thousand under Irvin McDowell marched 25 miles (40 km) south from Washington, DC, to Manassas Junction, where P. G. T. Beauregard was camped with twenty-two thousand Confederate soldiers. The two armies were equally inexperienced, so McDowell's larger force had the upper hand. But an army of ten thousand came to Beauregard's rescue, traveling 60 miles (97 km) from Harper's Ferry by rail. The speedy

Andrew Carnegie, Telegrapher and Railroad Man

The man once called "the richest man in the world" made his fortune in the technologies that won the Civil War. Andrew Carnegie (1835–1919) experienced firsthand the new developments in communication and transportation and recognized the potential of both the telegraph and the railroad.

Andrew Carnegie used his great wealth to enrich the lives of others, starting and giving to numerous charities.

A poor immigrant from Scotland, Carnegie landed his first job in the communications industry at about age fifteen. He worked as a messenger boy for the Ohio Telegraph Company office in Pittsburgh, Pennsylvania, delivering telegrams. As the coded signals came across the telegraph wires, they were marked on slips of paper and then translated into words. Carnegie learned to decipher the messages quickly by hearing the signals before they were transcribed. His skill earned him a promotion to operator. It also caught the attention of Thomas Scott, an agent of the Pennsylvania Railroad Company. Scott hired Carnegie as his personal secretary and telegraph operator. Thus by the time he was eighteen, Carnegie was employed in both of the technologies that would radically alter America.

When the Civil War began, President Lincoln appointed Scott assistant secretary of war in charge of military transportation. Scott brought Carnegie along as superintendent of the Union's railways and telegraph lines. In that capacity, he was responsible for building and repairing railroad track and stringing telegraph wire for the Union cause. Before the first major battle of the war, a telegraph wire he was working with snapped and sliced his cheek, leaving a permanent scar. He would always joke that he was the first casualty of the conflict.

With his understanding of the value of the new technologies and his connections at the Pennsylvania Railroad, Carnegie invested in several railroad-related enterprises. The investments eventually took him to the steel business and the founding of what is today the US Steel Corporation.

When Sherman's men destroyed Confederate railroads, they heated the rails and twisted them around poles and trees so they could not be repaired. People called them "Sherman's bowties" or "Sherman's neckties."

arrival of fresh troops turned the tide, enabling Beauregard to send the Union Army fleeing. Bull Run was just the first of many occasions on which the timely dispatch of reinforcements by rail turned struggles into victories for the South.

In addition to speed, transport of troops by railroads had another advantage over the older method of overland marches: rail cars could skirt opposing forces and bring armies straight to the battlefront. That is what Confederate general Braxton Bragg had in mind when he wanted to move his thirty thousand men from Tupelo, Mississippi, to Chattanooga, Tennessee, to prevent a Union takeover of that city. The direct route would have meant a 245-mile (394 km) march through Union-held territory. Instead he used the railroads. The troops traveled in a V formation: south to Mobile, Alabama, then north to Chattanooga. Even with changing railroads at least six times and crossing Mobile Bay by steamboat, they covered the 766 miles (1,233 km) in about two weeks—the same amount of time or less than it would have taken to march the shorter route. They arrived rested, safe, and able to surprise and rout their enemy.

THE TABLES TURN

The edge the railroads gave the South withered by the middle of 1863. The longer the war dragged on, the more use the rails received. Tracks wore out but Southern factories produced no replacement parts after 1861. To repair the lines critical to war supply, the Confederate government had to tear up rails from less important routes. In addition, Northern armies had captured some of the Southern lines and were able to put them to their own use. To keep the Union Army from taking advantage of the South's railroads, defeated Southern forces sometimes destroyed railroad tracks behind them as they fled.

The turning point was probably the series of battles for Chattanooga in September 1863. The railroads enabled the South to win the first round. The Confederates prevailed at Chickamauga when twelve thousand reinforcements came from Virginia, 800 miles (1,287 km) away. They had to use fourteen different railroads, and they made the journey in twelve days. But the victory did not last. Two weeks later, the Union transferred twenty-five thousand men from Virginia to the Chattanooga battlefield. They came on a longer route, covering 1,200 miles (1,931 km) on eight rail lines, arriving in twelve days. Trains also brought artillery and a massive amount of supplies, including mule teams, wagons, and horse ambulances. Such a feat would have been unthinkable without the railroads. With the additional men and materials, the Union was able to retake and hold Chattanooga.

From Chattanooga, Union general William Sherman launched his campaign to take Atlanta. He used some of the same deteriorating and damaged railroad lines that had brought the Confederates from Virginia, capturing them section by section as he moved south. He had ten thousand of his troops trained to repair the lines. To reach Atlanta, his men had to lay 75 miles (121 km) of new track and build eleven bridges.

Advancing deeper south, the Union Army strung telegraph lines as it went. The lines were connected to a small telegraph office in the War Department in Washington, DC. President Lincoln spent hours in that office, sending and receiving messages from the battle front. For the first time in history, the commander in chief provided strategic guidance to his generals in real time.

As Southern dominance in railroads declined, the number of Southern victories in battle also dropped. In just a few years, this technology never before used in a major war had become essential. Many other factors contributed to the outcome of the Civil War, but perhaps none as greatly as railroads.

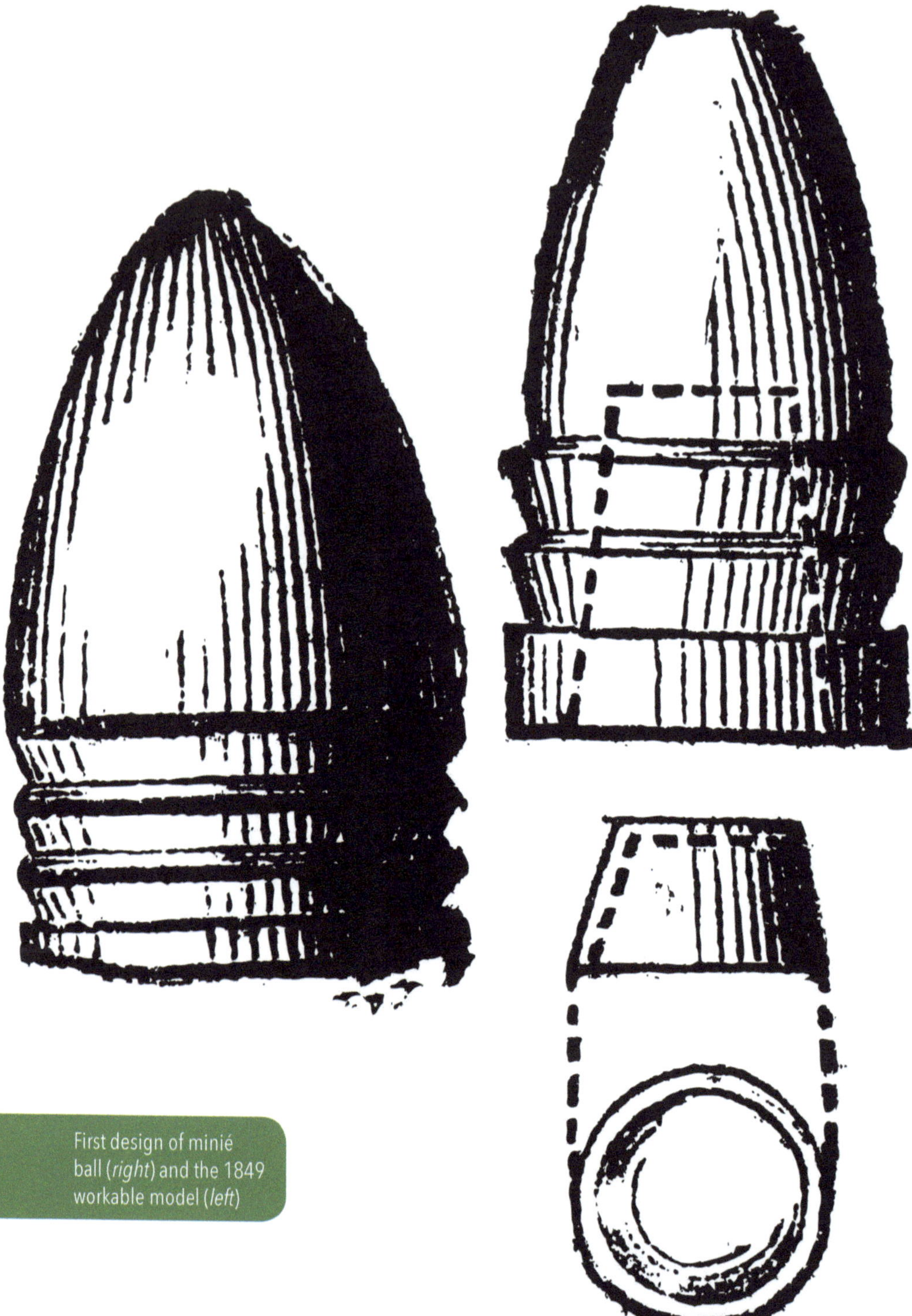

First design of minié ball (*right*) and the 1849 workable model (*left*)

CHAPTER FOUR

Barrels and Bullets

One of the greatest technological innovations to ever affect warfare was about the size of a quarter. It was only 1 inch (2.54 cm) long and weighed just over 1 ounce (28 grams). This very small item completely altered the way battles were fought. It made the rifle a deadlier and more brutal weapon. It changed where cannons were placed on a battlefield. It eliminated the volley formation, bayonets, and the cavalry charge. The minié bullet, which debuted in the Civil War, dictated the weapons and many of the tactics of the wars that followed.

THE PROBLEMS WITH GROOVES

The minié bullet solved the main problems with using the rifle in warfare. Rifles had been used in America by hunters and frontiersmen since before the American Revolution. Unlike the musket, they enabled shooters to aim at a precise target and hit it from 400 to 500 feet (122 to 152 m). But the very feature that made them effective—rifling—created problems when soldiers tried to use them in battle. The problem was not so much with the rifling as with the shot, the solid projectile fired from the weapon.

The shot for early rifles was the same as for muskets: a lead ball. In a rifle, the lead ball was about the same diameter as the bore of the barrel. It had to fit snugly so it would catch in the grooves and come straight out of the muzzle instead of at an angle. Every time the rifle was fired, some of the burnt powder clung to the sides of the bore, making the barrel a little smaller. After a few shots, the rifle had to be cleaned or the ball could not be loaded—not something that could be done in the middle of a firefight. What was needed seemed impossible: a projectile that was loose at loading but tight at firing.

FROM BALL TO BULLET

Such a projectile did exist. A British army captain found it in an ancient, primitive weapon: a blowgun. Captain John Norton, stationed in India in the 1830s, examined the darts tribal hunters loaded into their very simple but very effective weapons. The sharp darts were attached to a soft, spongy base. The base was made of pith, tissue from the insides of tree trunks. When the hunter blew into the gun, the air from the hunter's lungs expanded the pith so there was no space between the dart and the sides of the tube. The expandable base created a missile that was loose at loading but tight at firing.

Norton set out to adapt the concept to the rifles of England. Others improved on his basic design, and French army captain Claude-Étienne Minié came up with a workable model in 1849. His was the name given to the projectile. Hence the technology is properly called the "minié bullet" (pronounced min-YAY), but in America it is often called the "minie ball" (pronounced MI-nee), even though it was never a ball. The British government bought the rights to use the bullet and the world first saw its power in the Crimean War (1853–1856).

The minié ball was not a ball but a cone-shaped bullet. Its soft iron base was hollow. The idea was that when the weapon was fired, the skirting—the thin metal making up the hollow base—would flare outward, engaging the rifling. To make the skirting flare, Minié put an iron or wooden plug partway into the base. The gases from the charge pushed the plug into the hollow base, forcing the skirting out. The expanded base also prevented the gases from leaking out around the sides of the bullet, so all the force of the charge went into the bullet.

But the gases did not always push the plug out of the barrel with the bullet, and an accumulation of small plugs could clog the barrel. That problem was solved by James Burton, a worker in the armory at Harper's Ferry, then in Virginia. He lengthened the bullet slightly and made the metal of the skirting a little thinner. Those changes eliminated the need for a plug. Burton's minié ball was exactly what an infantryman needed: a bullet that slid easily into the barrel, sealed the gases behind it, and engaged the rifling. It could, therefore, be used in a weapon with a range of 1,500 yards (1,371 m) with deadly accuracy at up to 500 yards (457 m). The minié ball made the rifle effective and practical for military use.

The US Army adopted the minié bullet and the rifle musket in 1855. Ironically, the secretary of war who made that decision was Jefferson Davis, who six years later would be president of the Confederacy. The American manufacturing system was able to produce two million rifle muskets at the armory in Springfield, Massachusetts. The Springfield Model 1861 was the standard weapon of the Union infantry in the Civil War.

The South did not have the manufacturing capability of the North; the Confederacy had to purchase weapons from England. Over the course of the war, the South imported about four hundred thousand Enfield rifle muskets. Fortunately for the Confederacy, the minié ball fit both the Springfield and the Enfield, so when the Southerners captured Northern weapons, they were able to use them. Although a variety of implements were used in the Civil War (including lances!), the most common weapon of the infantryman of both North and South was the rifle musket with minié balls.

The Bullet and Rifle Reshape Warfare

The Civil War generals recognized the superiority of the minié bullet and rifle in range and accuracy, but they were slow to

William Greener

Claude-Étienne Minié gets the credit for inventing the minié ball, but he was not the first to produce such a bullet. The British gunmaker William Greener was thirteen years ahead of the Frenchman. Greener's projectile was an oval lead bullet. Greener drilled a hole in the bullet and inserted a tapered plug. As with the minié ball, the plug was forced into the ball when the gun was fired, expanding the ball against the rifling. Greener tried to sell his idea to the British Ordnance Department, but the officials rejected his design. They saw no advantage over the ammunition then in use, reasoning that a bullet that required two pieces would be more complicated and more expensive to manufacture than the simple lead ball.

Greener abandoned his creation and focused on other inventions—rifles, revolvers, and harpoon guns, among others. He won awards at international exhibitions in London, Paris, and New York. He invented an electric light, a new type of miner's lamp, a gate control for railroad crossings, and a lifeboat that righted itself if it capsized. But in 1852 when England purchased the patent from Minié for his bullet for £20,000 (about $2.6 million in 2015), Greener complained, arguing that he had the idea first. It took him five years to prove his case, but the British government finally acknowledged that Greener was right. It awarded him £1,000 (about $130,000 in 2015), not for his design but for "the first public suggestion of the principle of expansion, commonly called the Minié principle."

understand what the revolutionary technology meant for military tactics. They had new tools but old practices. The result was an incredibly high number of dead. Not until far into the conflict did the military leaders realize that the new weaponry would require new methods.

The tried and true start to battle had been the infantry attack. It was a frontal assault, a wall of muskets firing at a very similar

This mock Civil War scene depicts Union infantrymen after firing a volley at a similar line of Confederate re-enactors.

wall of defenders. The line of attackers marched to within about 100 yards (91 m) of the defenders, stood in massed formation, shouldered their weapons together on command, and fired a volley into the opposing line. The defenders waited for the enemy to come within range, then fired a volley into their line. The purpose of the frontal assault was to scatter the other side and seize the momentum. The tactic was often effective when the two sides were fairly evenly matched and everybody had muskets. But the rifle changed the balance. Its longer range allowed the defenders to fire into the advancing force before the attackers had a chance to ready their weapons. The gun's accuracy enabled the bullets to hit many targets in the closely packed lines. A frontal assault became a suicide mission, as so many battles of the Civil War demonstrate. The high casualty numbers of the war are primarily due to use of this outmoded tactic. Historians estimate that 90 percent of all battle injuries were inflicted with minié balls.

By the war's end, the rifle had altered the way foot soldiers fought. Gone were the infantry charge, the volley, and the bayonet attack. In their place were raids, small skirmishes before the main battles, and the beginning of trench warfare.

The cavalry was also impacted by the rifle. The mounted soldiers of the past stormed in after the opposing infantry had been overwhelmed and crushed them with their weapons and their horses' hooves. But the foot soldier with a rifle could shoot several times before horse and rider came close enough to do their job. The cavalry's role shifted. In the Civil War, the

This Winslow Homer drawing shows a surgeon (*front left*) at the rear of a battlefield. The man in the center is delivering supplies; an ambulance is seen in the background. The minié bullet inflicted far more serious injuries than the lead ball.

cavalry was used less for battle and more for small raids and **reconnaissance** missions.

The function of artillery also shifted. Because of the rifle, artillery became more useful for defense than for attack. The old tactic was to position batteries of six field pieces near the front in support of the advancing infantry. But the artillery pieces, like muskets and early rifles, were front-loaded. That made the cannoneers easy targets for foot soldiers with rifles. Simply moving the batteries back until they were out of rifle range was not a good option; it risked having the balls and shells land on their own infantry. Defenders, however, could place their heavy guns on higher ground and unleash their fire on the enemy below.

The generals of the Civil War had been schooled in the tactics of an earlier era. Those with battle experience had gotten it in the Mexican War (1846–1848). In that conflict, the old tactics, particularly the frontal assault, appeared to work. However, their opponents in that war had been poorly trained men equipped with muskets and lead balls. It is little wonder the generals did not immediately understand the tremendous difference the minié ball and rifle musket were to make. These twin innovations that eventually transformed military tactics remain the basis of the weapons and ammunition of today.

This image from 1864 shows the Battle of Mobile Bay.

CHAPTER FIVE

Wood and Iron

The Civil War actually began at sea. The first shots fired by the rebellious South were directed at a Union ship. They occurred on January 9, 1861, three months before the surrender of Fort Sumter.

Shortly after South Carolina announced its intention to secede, it seized three forts in Charleston harbor. A fourth fort—Sumter—was occupied by a small garrison of federal soldiers. South Carolina demanded the federal troops leave, but they refused. The stranded forces were running low on supplies. Not wanting to worsen the already tense standoff, the president decided to send both reinforcements and provisions on a civilian ship instead of a military vessel. When the *Star of the West* neared the fort, South Carolinians fired at the unarmed ship. The soldiers at Sumter did not return fire and the ship turned around and left without unloading its men or its cargo. War was averted for the moment, but the first cannons had sounded.

The Navies

Naval warfare was inevitable in the Civil War. The Confederacy's 3,500-mile (5,633 km) coastline practically invited attack. What really guaranteed battles on the sea was the South's dependency on foreign trade. If the Union could block the South's ports, it could cut off its primary supply line. Believing that he who controls the logistics of a war controls the outcome, the Union made a strategic decision to blockade the Southern ports.

When President Lincoln announced the blockade, the Union navy had forty-two usable warships. The Confederacy had none. Both sides immediately scrambled to acquire ships. The US Navy built, bought, or repurposed all kinds of vessels so that by the end of the war it had the largest fleet in the world: 671 ships. The South, with far fewer shipyards, cobbled together a much smaller navy.

Both navies benefited from the innovations of the Industrial Revolution. After Robert Fulton built the navy's first steam-powered ship in 1815, all the new warships used the technology. Many kept their sails also, conserving coal for only the occasions they needed steam. Nineteenth-century warships had tall masts and short smokestacks. The steam engines did not make the boats much faster, but they allowed them to be operated in any weather. The greatest advantage of steam over sails was that it permitted the ships to be maneuvered much more easily.

The industrial inventors had also produced new naval weapons. By 1860, shipboard cannons could shoot farther and more precisely than ever before. They also shot more destructive ammunition. Older guns lobbed iron balls on the decks of enemy vessels, crippling crews and knocking out masts. The new weapons fired shells packed with explosives. These ripped giant holes in the sides of the wooden boats.

IRONCLADS

It was just a matter of time before someone would think to cover the wooden sides of warships with iron. That someone was Napoleon III of France, nephew of Napoleon I. After the Crimean War, the emperor had a wooden ship built and its hull plated with iron. The *Gloire*, launched in 1859, withstood the strongest firepower of its day. Not to be outdone, Britain constructed a warship with its hull not plated but made of iron. The two rival nations spent the next few years in a competition to produce the strongest and best iron ship. Before long, Austria, Italy, Russia, and Spain had also joined the contest. But Europe was at relative peace. The first battle between ironclads would be in America.

The Confederacy, desperate to break the Union blockade of its ports, looked to add armored warships to its tiny fleet. Without sufficient resources to build new boats, the South created ironclads from whatever wooden ships they could find. They rebuilt the decks and clad, or covered, the decks and the sides above the waterline with iron. The first ironclad in America was the CSS (for Confederate State Ship) *Manassas*.

The *Manassas* was a small steamboat, originally an icebreaker. Its iron-plated deck was curved, like a turtle's back, so any cannonball that landed on it would roll off into the water. It carried only one gun, but on its bow was a pointed iron ram. Sent as part of a small fleet to drive the Union blockaders from the mouth of the Mississippi River, the *Manassas* was the first ironclad to be used in the war. In October 1861, the boat managed to ram a Union ship but did not do it much damage. The turtle back was successful in repelling enemy fire, but the *Manassas* lost its ram and its smokestack and had one of its engines temporarily disabled. Six months later it ran aground in battle, caught fire, and sank.

THE CSS *VIRGINIA*

The South's most famous ironclad began as a Union battleship. When the war broke out, it was docked at the navy yard in Portsmouth, Virginia. After joining the Confederacy, Virginia took over the shipyard. The evacuating federal troops tried to take the **frigate** *Merrimack*, a mid-sized warship, with them as they left, but the rebels blocked them. To keep the Southerners from using the boat against them, they set it on fire and sank what remained of it.

As the Union blockade tightened and the war supplies of the South slowly dwindled, the secretary of the Confederate Navy scoured his shipyards for ways to bolster his forces. He did not have the manufacturing resources to build steam engines to repair old boats. He thought of the *Merrimack* and wondered if its engine could be salvaged. He raised the scuttled wreck and examined the damage. Only the parts above the waterline were burnt; the rest of the hull was intact. The engine and other machinery were in poor but working condition. Enough of the ship remained to convert it to new use.

The charred wood was cut off and replaced with a new deck. Instead of a turtle back like the *Manassas*, a **casemate**—an enclosure for armaments—was placed atop the deck. The casemate and sides were clad with two layers of 2-inch (5 cm) plates of iron; the armor was 4 inches (10 cm) thick. The ship was outfitted with ten guns. The builders knew the Union would also make ironclads, and they knew their weapons would not be able to penetrate the armor of another ship with iron sides, so they added an iron ram to the bow; it could tear holes in the unprotected wooden part of a hull below the waterline. They christened the new ship the CSS *Virginia* (although many historians still call it the *Merrimack*; some use the erroneous spelling *Merrimac*). By March 1862, it was ready to challenge the Union blockade.

THE USS *MONITOR*

By the time word reached Washington that the South was converting the *Merrimack* to a steam-powered ironclad, the work was nearly complete. Congress hurriedly called for designs for an armored warship. The contract was awarded to the Swedish-born inventor John Ericsson, and he was given one hundred days to build the boat. With many factories contributing parts and labor and Ericsson personally overseeing the work, the project was miraculously finished on time. The result was a vessel unlike any seen before.

The boat, dubbed the USS *Monitor*, was revolutionary in many ways; it contained forty freshly patented devices. It looked more like

A Persistent Inventor

John Ericsson (1803–1889) was drawing designs since at least his teens. At twelve he worked with his father, making maps for a cross-country canal in his native Sweden. By age fifteen he had been made a surveyor for the canal project. At seventeen he joined the Swedish army, in which he served as an engineer and mapmaker. He moved to England and then to America and became a US citizen in 1848.

Ericsson was a tireless inventor. He received awards for his creations of a deep-sea distance finder, a steam fire extinguisher, and an engine that used hot air instead of steam. However, many of his inventions, though recognized as ingenious, did not meet with success. Sometimes that was because he simply could not sell his idea. The British Admiralty was not interested in his plan for a steamship with a screw propeller, a design that eventually became the norm for steamships. France rejected his bid to build an ironclad with a revolving gun turret. He built his steamship for the US Navy, but after a tragic explosion on the ship, the navy refused to give him another chance for seventeen years.

When the call came for designs for an armored battleship, Ericsson was convinced his *Monitor* was what the country needed. He bypassed the navy officials and submitted his proposal directly to Abraham Lincoln. The fears and mistrust of the officials were outweighed by the fact that the president liked Ericsson's drawings. The rest is history.

The two-day Battle of Hampton Roads was the worst in US naval history until Pearl Harbor in 1941. The battle is best remembered for the fight between the *Monitor* (*center foreground*) and the *Virginia* (*right foreground*).

a raft than a warship. Newspapers ridiculed it, calling it a "cheese box on a raft." It sat low in the water, its deck only 18 inches (46 cm) above the waterline. In the center of the deck was a gun turret—the "cheese box"—9 feet (2.7 m) tall and plated with 8 inches (20 cm) of iron. The sides of the raft had 3 to 5 inches (8 to 13 cm) of iron plate. The turret revolved so the guns could fire in any direction.

The *Monitor* was about 100 feet (30 m) shorter than the *Virginia* and 3,000 tons (2,722 metric tons) lighter. It carried only two guns to the *Virginia*'s ten and had no ram. It could operate with only 49 men, whereas the *Virginia* required 320. It could probably sink a wooden ship, but what could it do against another, much larger ironclad? The world found out March 9, 1862.

THE BATTLE OF HAMPTON ROADS

The day before, the *Virginia* had made its first move. Its target was a fleet of five Union blockaders anchored in the harbor of Hampton Roads, Virginia. The ironclad first attacked the twenty-four-gun *Cumberland*, pounding it with gunfire and ramming its wooden hull. As the Union ship sank, the *Virginia* turned its guns toward the larger frigate, the *Congress*. While the shells from the *Congress* bounced off the iron sides of the *Virginia*'s casemate, hot shot—heated balls—from the *Virginia* set fire to the wooden frigate. It burned for hours and finally exploded and went down. A third Union ship, the *Minnesota*, ran aground in an attempt to escape. Nightfall kept the ironclad from finishing off the *Minnesota*; that job could wait until morning.

However, morning held a surprise for the crew of the *Virginia*. When the Confederate boat approached the disabled *Minnesota*, firing as it neared, a strange shape emerged and blocked its path. The guns of the *Monitor* then fired the opening round of the first battle between ironclads. The ships fought for four hours, the *Virginia* hurling shells and the *Monitor* lobbing solid shot. The vessels fought at close range, even colliding at times. The *Virginia* tried to ram the *Monitor*, but its battle with the *Cumberland* had damaged its ram. Some of the shots inflicted minor damage, but nothing of consequence. The crews decided that continued fighting was a waste of ammunition. The *Virginia* left, unable to sink the Union ship but also unable to be sunk. The *Monitor* did not pursue the Confederate vessel, having succeeded in its mission of protecting the harbor. The battle was essentially a draw.

TURNING POINT

In the months that followed the Battle of Hampton Roads, "*Monitor* fever" swept the North. Factories throughout the Northeast began constructing small, flat warships according to Ericsson's design. They turned out sixty boats whereas the South, also caught up in the building frenzy, was able to clad only about twenty old wooden vessels with iron.

The new warships were not only invincible against explosive shells, but they were also able to navigate shallow waters. Some became part of the Union's "**brown navy**," the riverboats that blockaded and attacked Southern ports up and down the Mississippi. They were instrumental in the Union's successful strategy to control the river, splitting the Confederacy in two.

Although neither the *Virginia* nor the *Monitor* fought again after the Battle of Hampton Roads, the clash of the ironclads was the most significant event in all of naval military history up to that time. It rendered the guns of coastal forts utterly useless, unable to penetrate ships' armor. It forced officers to rethink the tactics of naval warfare. It demonstrated the overwhelming superiority of steam-powered iron battleships over wooden sailing vessels. In one engagement, the type of ships that had ruled the seas for centuries became obsolete. From that point on, every new warship was made of iron or steel.

The train station at Hanover Junction, Pennsylvania, in 1863. The man in the stovepipe hat may—or may not—be Abraham Lincoln, who stopped here on his way to deliver the Gettysburg Address.

CHAPTER SIX

After the War

The Civil War is sometimes called both the last ancient war and the first modern war. It employed philosophies and practices of medieval armies side by side with inventions that had never before been imagined. Some Civil War soldiers actually fought with pikes and others used an early version of the machine gun. Some supplies arrived at the front by mule train and some by rail car. Naval battles were waged from sailing ships as well as submarines. The Civil War occurred at a time America was moving from a nation of farmers to a manufacturing giant. The war was partially shaped by that shift, and it also helped fuel it.

The period from about 1840 until roughly the beginning of World War I was actually a second industrial revolution. The first had to do with manufacturing; the second, with technology. In the first, the method of producing goods changed from hand to machines. It was a change in thinking, in ways of doing things. In the second, the thinking and methods were improved through an explosion in technological innovation. People created new and better machines and processes. In 1844 the US Patent Office issued 1,045 patents on new inventions; in the thirty years following the Civil War it issued at least 15,000 each year.

The Civil War took place in the middle of the technological boom that was the second industrial revolution. Its leaders had the benefit of some of the new technologies and the opportunities to refine them. Some were short-lived oddities, such as hydrogen-filled balloons used for aerial reconnaissance. Others were major factors in the outcome of the war and led to even more revolutionary advancements. A number of those innovations had major impacts outside the military realm; they made huge differences in ways people lived and worked for years to come. Among the technologies that influenced both the war and society were the railroad, the minié ball, and ironclad ships.

RAILROADS SHAPE MILITARY TACTICS

The Civil War showed that railroads, in addition to being huge logistical benefits, frequently dictated military tactics. As vital supply channels, rail lines were easier to attack than wagon trains. Soldiers did not have to find the supplies to keep them from getting to an entrenched enemy; all they had to do was derail the train. If their intelligence told them their opponents' route, they could send a few soldiers to rip up tracks anywhere along the route, blocking the supply without even encountering the enemy.

The trains could take troops only as far as a **railhead**, a spot where railway lines began or ended. At that point the men had to unload their artillery and ammunition as well as the wagons and animals that would take the equipment to the battlefield. Because the commanders did not want to be far from their supplies, armies tended to congregate near the railheads and battles were fought close to rail lines. This tactic made surprise attacks difficult to pull off. On the other hand, railroads also allowed units to be dispatched hundreds of miles from one theater to another very quickly, overwhelming enemy forces and catching them off guard.

Cities that were rail centers, where different rail lines met, were prime military targets. They were important not only for military transport but mainly because they were essential to the region's economy. Military strategy had always been to capture such cities, but their dependence on railroads gave commanders a new tactic for doing so. If an army could sever the rail lines to a city, it could starve the city into surrender. That is exactly how General William T. Sherman took Atlanta and began his famous march to the sea.

Some historians believe the railroads made the war last longer. When an army lost a battle, if the soldiers could get to their trains and escape instead of surrendering, they did so, or they fell back a short distance, waited for reinforcements, and joined the battle again. That tactic meant campaigns that otherwise might have ended dragged on. The South did not surrender until the

Union Army won control of the railroad line that supplied General Robert E. Lee's Confederate forces.

RAILROADS OPEN THE WEST

When the war was over, the country turned its attention not to the North or the South but to the West. Vast areas beyond the Mississippi awaited fulfillment of the country's manifest destiny, and the railroads would be instrumental in that process. The Civil War did not start railroad construction in the West; the first, very short lines of track were laid in 1855. The expansion of railroads westward had stalled, however, and the war got the building started again.

In the 1850s, Americans dreamed of a transcontinental railroad, a system that would stretch from the eastern network of track to the Pacific Ocean. It would permit the businesses in the East to spread into new territory. But people disagreed on where the railroad should be built. Northern politicians wanted the lines to go through the Free States and Southerners wanted a southern route. The primary reason for the 1854

At the Golden Spike ceremony, Leland Sanford of the Central Pacific Railroad drove a railroad spike into the ground at Promontory Point, Utah, joining his railroad with the Union Pacific.

The Great Railroad Strike of 1877

The boom in the railroad industry came crashing to a halt in July 1877. A huge depression, overbuilding, and other financial woes were eating into the profits of railroad companies. One by one, the big companies began repeatedly reducing the pay, cutting the hours, and increasing the workload of their workers. The actions led to America's first large labor strike.

It began when forty locomotive firemen of the Baltimore and Ohio Railroad walked off their jobs. Workers at stations in West Virginia and Maryland shut down the trains, demanding their pay be restored. The work stoppage spread to other railroads and to cities in Pennsylvania, Ohio, Kentucky, Illinois, and Missouri. Many of the protests escalated into riots. Strikers threw rocks, looted depots, and set fire to buildings and rail cars. Laborers in iron and steel mills and other industries joined the railroad workers in sympathy with their cause. Demonstrations grew as large as twenty thousand people in Pittsburgh and Chicago.

State militias and National Guard units armed with rifles, bayonets, and Gatling guns were called to stop the demonstrations. In some cities, the soldiers fired into the crowds. The riots lasted only a few weeks, but in that time, half of the country's freight and one hundred thousand railroad workers sat idle. More than a hundred people were killed, and millions of dollars of property was destroyed. The strike was finally stopped when President Rutherford B. Hayes, claiming he had to protect the US mail, sent federal troops to the turbulent cities.

Gadsden Purchase of parts of what are now Arizona and New Mexico was to secure land for a southern railway route. The route had to be settled in Congress because no private company could build the line. It would take help—land and partial funding—from the federal government. However, the lawmakers could not agree. The sectionalism that divided the country kept the western railroad from being built.

When the Southern states seceded, the legislators who remained in Congress easily agreed on a route. In 1862, they passed the Pacific Railway Act that allocated money for the project. However, the workers and materials required for building the line were channeled to the more critical war effort. Construction on the transcontinental railroad was delayed until after the war.

The war spurred railroad building in another way. It made government officials keenly aware of the problem of different gauges. The transcontinental railroad was to be built by two different companies, and other, smaller companies would eventually connect their lines to it. The government required the new railroad to place its tracks 4 feet 8.5 inches (1.4 m) apart, and this became the standard gauge that all other companies adopted.

In 1869, the railway was completed. Settlers poured into the West, cities sprang up, and transcontinental trade grew. From east to west, states were tied economically.

NEW WEAPONS EMERGE

The railroad was the technology that probably had the greatest impact on the Civil War generals as they planned their strategies, but for the soldier in the field, the most important innovations were weapons technologies. The typical infantryman began the war with a single-shot, muzzle-loaded, shoulder-fired weapon, either a smoothbore or rifled musket. Over the four years of the conflict, he may have progressed to breechloaders and repeaters.

The concept of loading a firearm from the breech was not new in the 1860s; breechloaders had been around since the Revolutionary War. However, the US Army did not use them for a number of reasons. When he was still Secretary of War, Jefferson Davis explained why. He noted that the primary advantage of the breechloader was that it was easy to load, but once the minié ball was introduced, loading from the muzzle was almost as easy. Davis cited a number of disadvantages. Breechloaders were more complex and therefore more expensive. They broke down more frequently and were difficult to repair. They required special ammunition. Their only value, he concluded, was for cavalry, who could not easily load from the muzzle. So, when the war began, only the cavalry were issued breechloaders.

But another revolutionary technology introduced in the 1840s made breechloaders practical for every rifleman: the metal bullet cartridge. The cartridge combined the three essentials for firing a weapon—powder, primer, and projectile—in one compact package. Unlike paper or cloth cartridges that held

This unidentified soldier was probably in a Union cavalry unit. He holds a breech-loading carbine, a Colt revolver, and a cavalry sword.

only powder and projectile, the metal cartridge held everything needed for loading. It had the bonus benefit of being waterproof. Instead of firing three rounds per minute, an infantryman with a breechloader could now fire twenty.

Gunmakers continued to refine their products. They devised ways to place several cartridges into a magazine that fed the cartridges into a weapon's breech. The result was the repeater, a weapon that could fire more than one bullet before needing to be reloaded. By 1863, several multiple-shot weapons were available. The first were made by Sharps: a rifle as well as a **carbine**—a light, short-barreled rifle. Spencer developed seven-shot rifles and carbines that could empty their magazines in thirty seconds, and Henry made a sixteen-shot repeater.

People in the War Department debated the merits of repeaters. Many feared their rapid fire would result in wasted ammunition. Others were impressed with their speed and accuracy; some could fire twenty shots a minute. In the end, thousands of the new weapons made their way to the field before the war ended. The Union purchased ninety-five thousand Spencer carbines, the most popular repeater.

Weapons development continued throughout and after the war. One of the most innovative firearms of the period was created by Richard Gatling. Named after him, the Gatling gun was basically the first machine gun. Gatling was not able to sell his invention to the Union Army, but one general purchased twelve for his men

This captured *David*, one of more than twenty spar torpedo boats modeled after the CSS *David*, was designed to cripple the "Goliath"—the Union naval blockade.

and used them successfully at the Battle of Petersburg in 1864. For all its novelty—revolving barrels, automatic loading, 150-round-per-minute capability—the Gatling gun, like all the weapons technology of the Civil War, used a version of the minié ball.

UNDERWATER WEAPONS

Just as Civil War weapons advanced to more and more sophisticated forms, the naval machinery of the period progressed to meet the challenges on the water. The revolutionary technology of the ironclad was the beginning of a number of naval innovations. The South, strangled by the Union blockade and unable to build enough ships to counter the Union's fleet, was forced to come up with novel devices.

Since cannons could not pierce the ironclads' above-water plating, Confederate engineers had to find a way to blow holes in their wooden hulls below the water. They came up with what they called torpedoes, which were actually mines. Torpedoes were often artillery shells fitted with a fuse that would cause them to explode upon contact. They were placed in rivers or narrow channels leading into harbors.

The South devised a variety of torpedoes. Some floated on the top of the water and others were hidden below the surface—mounted on poles, set on wooden frames, or chained to weights. Some were remotely detonated using electricity, a technology relatively new in the 1860s. An electric charge was what hit the USS *Cairo* in December 1862, the first ironclad to be sunk by a mine.

These mines were defensive weapons. For offense, the Confederate Navy created the spar torpedo. The device was attached to a spar, a long pole, and delivered to its target by a specially designed boat. When the cigar-shaped boat neared the enemy ship, it allowed special tanks on board to fill with water, submerging the boat almost completely. Its crew then exploded the torpedo against its target. The torpedoes were so effective that the South took the next logical step, building a submarine to launch them. On its first run in 1864, the *Hunley* became the first submarine to sink a ship of war. However, the *Hunley* also sank in the process.

As the success and the failure of the *Hunley* shows, the many innovations that came out of the Civil War were not perfect, fully complete products. They were steps in the evolutionary process of technological development. They came about in response to imperfect inventions of the past and they laid the foundation for better creations in the future. The technologies that had such great impact in the Civil War have continued to evolve and, in some form or another, are still with us today.

Both sides in World War I depended heavily on railroads. These British soldiers were transported by light railway to a battle in Belgium.

CHAPTER SEVEN

Civil War Technology Today

People make changes because they feel a need. That's what the expression "Necessity is the mother of inventions" means. The three major new technologies of the Civil War, as well as many smaller ones, were created or advanced because of the needs of war. The railroad's growth into a giant industry occurred because military officers needed reliable transportation. The minié ball and rifle came about because soldiers needed effective weapons. Ironclads were developed because the Confederate Navy needed battleships. These technological innovations arose from necessity.

As new circumstances give rise to new needs, inventions are either refined so they meet the current need or they disappear as some new innovation fits the bill better. The railroad, the minié ball, and the ironclad are among the technologies that have survived and continue to impact modern life.

THE IMPACT OF RAILROADS

For at least eighty years after the Civil War, railroads remained important factors in large-scale wars. In World War I, Germany's carefully calculated plan depended on trains to transport troops from the western to the eastern front. In World War II, railroads were the supply lines as well as strategic objectives for both sides. American railroads were critical in the war effort, moving materials and personnel across the country for battle overseas. However, after World War II, with modern roads, truck convoys, and air transport, railroads were no longer the best option for war transport.

By that time, railroads had also lost much of their appeal in society. Americans preferred the automobile and airplane to passenger trains. Moving freight by train had become unprofitable because of competition from trucks using interstate highways and heavy government regulation of railroads. Railroad use declined steadily, and in the 1970s, many companies, including those that had carried troops in the Civil War, could no longer stay in business. Railroads were on the brink of extinction. To attract business, they had to find needs they could fill.

There was a need was for high-speed passenger travel between cities, but providing that service would require updating aging cars, installing heating and lighting systems in the cars, purchasing new equipment, repairing outdated stations, and establishing new routes. No company had the money to do all that, so the federal government stepped in to help. In 1970, Congress passed the Rail Passenger Service Act, removing the regulation that kept passenger and freight service coupled together. It also created Amtrak, a company providing intercity passenger service.

Just as the government partnered with railroad companies in the 1860s to build the transcontinental railroad, today Amtrak is funded by the federal government. It connects five hundred communities from coast to coast and into Canada. Responding to the demand for high-speed passenger service, its trains travel at an average of 125 miles per hour (201 kilometers per hour). The Acela Express, Amtrak's line in the busy northeast corridor between Washington, DC, and Boston, can reach speeds of 150 miles per hour (241 kmh). The company is constantly exploring options for trains that can go even faster, are lighter and therefore consume less fuel, and cause less wear on tracks. Despite ongoing financial challenges and competition from highway and air modes of travel, Amtrak's millions of customers suggest that passenger trains are here to stay.

Where the railroad came roaring back from the edge of disaster was in the area of freight hauling. The problem was not a lack of need but government regulation that made competing with other forms of transportation nearly impossible. When Congress removed most of those regulations through the Staggers Rail Act of 1980, the railroads began to innovate to recapture business.

Amtrak calls its train service in the busy northeast corridor "Acela Express" to remind users of two features of the rail service. "Acela" is a combination of "excellence" and "acceleration."

They developed unit trains for rapid shipping of single products short distances. They replaced boxcars with flatcars that can hold intermodal containers, containers that can be moved between different transportation modes without disturbing their contents. Businesses that ship goods from one country to another often use intermodal containers. The container will come in to a port on a ship, travel a long distance by rail, and reach its final destination by truck. Rail companies built double-stack container cars that enable them to carry twice the load for the same cost. The continued technological innovation has brought railroads back to life and keeps them moving full steam—or rather, diesel—ahead.

WEAPONS

Like railroads, Civil War weapons technology has continued into the present day. Innovations have been made over the years as gunmakers have responded to the changing demands of new forms of warfare, but the minié ball and the rifled gun remain the bases for the bullets, artillery shells, and firearms manufactured today. The standard weapon for US infantry in World War II, the Garand M-1 rifle, and in the Vietnam War, the M16 assault rifle, had newer firing mechanisms but the same basic design as the Springfield rifle used at Gettysburg.

One of the great technologies coming out of World War II is an example of application of the old designs to new problems. The problem was air combat. The proximity fuse, also called the variable time or VT fuse, began as an antiaircraft device. The fuse is a sensor placed in the nose of an artillery shell. The sensor detects when the shell is within a set range of a target and triggers the shell to explode at that point. The very effective antiaircraft projectile, shot from a rifled gun, is basically a tiny radar in the cone of a giant minié ball.

Many twenty-first-century weapons are also essentially innovative additions to the rifle and the bullet that evolved from the minié ball. Most were designed for close-range, urban warfare.

Modern Urban Railroads

Rapid transit systems are becoming increasingly popular with commuters in large cities. In addition to speed, they offer freedom from driving, parking, and accidents.

The growth and decline of urban transit mirrored the rise and fall of the railroads. City rail transit began in the 1830s as carriages pulled by horses over metal rails. It progressed in 1873 to cable cars powered by steam rather than horses. Then came streetcars operated by electricity delivered through an overhead wire. By 1900, every large city and many small ones had electric railways for urban transit. Some extended the lines into outlying areas and a few linked to other cities. Some cities, such as New York and Chicago, built elevated railways on structures above the streets. Others, like Boston and Philadelphia, put electric rails beneath the ground in subways.

Streetcars suffered the same fate as railroads and were replaced by cars and buses. In the 1970s, urban rail transit saw a resurgence similar to that of the railroads. The need that spurred the rebirth was congestion and pollution caused by so many automobiles. Transit engineers adopted two technologies: rapid transit and light rail. Rapid transit works well in metropolitan areas that are spread out. The electric trains travel on rails completely segregated from all other traffic, often underground, and riders get on and off at stations. The trains can reach speeds of 70 miles per hour (113 kmh). Light rail systems are slower because they operate mostly within large cities rather than between communities. Counting time for stops, their average speed is about 20 to 25 miles per hour (32 to 40 kmh). Something like high-tech streetcars, they run on track in city streets or in the medians of the streets. Although the track is in city streets, it is separated from other traffic. Because of the benefits of these technologies—relief from traffic congestion, clean air, comfortable ride, good speed, convenience, and dependability—US cities are building more urban railroads.

The SCAR (Special Operations Forces Combat Assault Rifle) has barrels of 18-, 14-, and 10-inch (46, 36, and 25.4 cm) lengths that can be interchanged quickly in the field to accommodate rapidly changing conditions. Some shells have microchips that trigger detonation at specific distances, enabling soldiers to explode them in midair above targets hiding behind barricades. Some rifles are hinged and equipped with cameras and laser aiming devices so they can hit targets around corners. Others, like the FMG9 (Folding Machine Gun), can fit in a soldier's pocket.

The modern use of Civil War weapons technology is not limited to the military. Law enforcement, sports, and recreational firearms all continue to use rifled weapons and minié ball–based bullets. These technologies are what enable detectives to trace bullets to specific guns. The rifling in a gun's barrel is specific to the gun's make and model. That is, the grooves in the bore of a particular model have a distinct pattern and direction that impress themselves on the bullet as it moves through the barrel. Detectives can thus match a bullet to a firearm brand and model. Because the process of cutting the rifling into the barrel is not absolutely smooth, each rifle is unique and leaves markings on bullets unique to that weapon. All bullets fired from a specific gun have identical markings. Therefore, firing test bullets from a suspected weapon confirms whether the bullet in question came from that gun.

In sports weapons, current innovations focus not on the bullet or the barrel but on the sights. The future of hunting rifles may be in ballistic-solution sighting systems. **Ballistics** is the study of

The AR15 assault rifle is a modular weapons system, which means parts can be interchanged and components added to suit the needs and preferences of the operator and the situation.

bullets as they move, and ballistic-solution sighting systems enable shooters to calculate every conceivable factor that could affect the bullet's path and performance. These scopes use laser rangefinders and computers to home in on their targets. They measure external variables: temperature, air pressure, wind direction and drift, and distance to the target. They account for the specifics of the firearm that influence the bullet's trajectory: length of the barrel; rate and direction of the twist of the rifling; muzzle velocity; and the fractions of seconds it takes to lock, ignite, and eject the bullet. Shooting with pinpoint precision appears to be the future of sports weapon technology.

In law enforcement, the trend is toward less lethal weapons. Many so-called "nonlethal" weapons have actually resulted in a surprising number of deaths. TASER guns; rubber, wax, and plastic bullets; and chemical sprays can be lethal even when used correctly and carefully. For riot control, police departments are experimenting with weapons that emit sounds and odors so obnoxious they can cripple combatants. To stop individual attackers, they are examining pistol attachments that slow and weaken the impact of bullets. These attachments function much like airbags in cars, encapsulating the bullet so it slams against but not into its target. Although nothing powerful enough to stop an attacker can be truly nonlethal, the future of police weapons technology may be not in the firearm but in the bullet.

STEEL SHIPS

In the naval arena, Civil War technology evolved quickly from ironclad rams to steel battleships. Advancements in ship design, propulsion, and armaments made the battleships bigger, stronger, and faster, but the basic Civil War innovation of armored vessels has been the standard for warships since 1862.

However, the big, heavily armed battleship is becoming a relic of the past. The large guns of the battleship have been replaced with guided weapons that can be delivered by aircraft and submarines. The warship of the future may be a return to another technology of the ironclad: the stealth attacker. The ironclads were designed specifically to be low in the water in order to avoid detection. They were to sneak up on their targets and release their weapons, whether artillery shell, torpedo, or ram. The battleships of today's navy may be just such stealth vessels.

The *Zumwalt*-class stealth destroyer is one of the US Navy's newest warships. Although it is large, its stealth technology makes it appear on radar to be no larger than a fishing boat. It is armed with guided missiles as well as guns that can fire ten rounds per minute and hit a target 80 miles (129 km) away. It is a multi-mission ship, equipped for undersea warfare, ship-to-ship combat, and long-range attack of land targets. This futuristic battleship is an extremely high-tech version of Civil War naval technologies: equipped with underwater missile launchers instead of torpedoes and clad with stealth capability instead of iron. Some have commented that it looks like an ironclad.

Stealth was also the goal of another Civil War naval technology, the submarine. While the Civil War ship *Hunley* was created only to attack and destroy enemy vessels, the modern submarine is far more versatile. In addition to fighting surface ships and other submarines, its roles include controlling access to various parts of the ocean, protecting aircraft carriers and other military ships, laying mines, collecting intelligence, rescuing stranded soldiers and airmen, and secretly transporting and landing Special Operations forces. Submarines also attack land targets with cruise missiles. They have come a long way from planting spar torpedoes!

A tugboat helps move the just-built USS *Zumwalt* out of dry dock in preparation for service. The ultramodern guided missile destroyer is the first of three ships of its class.

1000

US society has come a long way in the century and a half since the Civil War. We have come from an industrializing economy to a leader in global production, from a population of 31.4 million to more than ten times that number, from a divided nation to an international power. We have advanced from horse-drawn carriages to supersonic transports, from Morse code to Unicode, from crossing the Mississippi to landing on the moon. The progress has come as individuals have responded creatively to needs, inventing new products and new ways of doing things. Great needs often give birth to great innovations. The Civil War, probably the largest upheaval of US history, was responsible for the development of three technologies, among others, that continue to shape society today.

GLOSSARY

abolitionist A person who believes that the practice of slavery should be completely stopped; a supporter of the movement to accomplish this end.

antebellum A term meaning "before a war"; usually refers to the time and events immediately preceding the American Civil War, generally from around 1800 to 1860. Some historians date it more narrowly, from 1812 to 1860.

ballistics The science of bodies in motion, specifically bullets in flight.

bore The inside of the barrel of a gun.

brown navy A fleet of warships used for naval operations in rivers. The word "brown" refers to river water, shallower than ocean water and muddied by sediment.

caliber The measure of the diameter of the bore, or inside, of a gun barrel or of a bullet; expressed in inches.

carbine A firearm with a barrel shorter than that of a typical rifle, usually under 20 inches (51 centimeters) long, and generally lighter than a typical rifle.

casemate An armored enclosure on the deck of a ship for housing guns.

Deep South The southeast region of the United States that encompasses the states of Alabama, Georgia, Louisiana, Mississippi, and North and South Carolina. Parts of Virginia, Tennessee, Arkansas, Texas, and Florida are sometimes included.

Free State A state in the United States in which slavery was prohibited by law.

frigate In the eighteenth and nineteenth centuries, a mid-sized, three-mast, square-sailed warship. Some frigates were powered by steam in addition to sails.

logistics The science of getting, storing, and transporting personnel, equipment, and supplies for a military operation.

manifest destiny A belief of nineteenth-century Americans that the destiny, or right, of America was to extend from the Atlantic to the Pacific Ocean.

railhead The point at which a railroad line began or ended.

reconnaissance A military strategy in which soldiers survey an enemy's area or people before attack.

repeater A firearm capable of loading multiple cartridges so more than one shot can be fired before the firearm requires reloading.

rifling A system of spiral grooves along the inside of a gun barrel.

secede To withdraw from. Secession is the formal act by which the Confederate states declared that they were no longer part of the United States.

strategy An overall plan to achieve an objective. Military strategy encompasses planning, coordinating, and directing operations to achieve a specific military goal.

tactics The steps in a strategy. Military tactics involve the placement and use of troops and weapons to implement a strategy.

Union A term referring to the United States, especially denoting the states allied against the Confederate states during the Civil War.

BIBLIOGRAPHY

Atherton, Kelsey D. "Inside the Zumwalt Destroyer." *Popular Science*, November 21, 2013. Accessed August 21, 2015. http://www.popsci.com/article/technology/inside-zumwalt-destroyer.

Baida, Peter. "Eli Whitney's Other Talent." *American Heritage* 38, no. 4 (1987). Accessed July 28, 2015. http://www.americanheritage.com/content/eli-whitney%E2%80%99s-other-talent?page=show.

"Civil War and Industrial Expansion, 1860–1897 (Overview)." *Gale Encyclopedia of US Economic History*, 1999. Retrieved August 13, 2015. http://www.encyclopedia.com/doc/1G2-3406400169.html.

Confederate States of America. *Declaration of the Immediate Causes Which Induce and Justify the Secession of South Carolina from the Federal Union.* Accessed July 27, 2015. http://avalon.law.yale.edu/19th_century/csa_scarsec.asp.

Gabel, Christopher R. *Railroad Generalship: Foundations of Civil War Strategy.* Fort Leavenworth, KS: Combat Study Institute Press, 1997. Accessed August 2, 2015. http://usacac.army.mil/cac2/cgsc/carl/download/csipubs/gabel4.pdf.

———. *Rails to Oblivion: The Battle of Confederate Railroads in the Civil War.* Fort Leavenworth, KS: Combat Study Institute Press, 2002. Accessed August 5, 2015. http://usacac.army.mil/cac2/cgsc/carl/download/csipubs/gabel6.pdf.

Howey, Allan W. "Weaponry: The Rifle-Musket and the Minié Ball." *Civil War Times*, October 1999. Accessed August 8, 2015. http://www.historynet.com/Minie-ball.

Killblane, Richard E. *Circle the Wagons: The History of US Army Convoy Security*. Fort Leavenworth, KS: Combat Studies Institute Press. Accessed August 3, 2015. http://carl.army.mil/download/csipubs/killblane.pdf.

Koenig, Alan R. "Railroad's Critical Role in the Civil War." *America's Civil War*, September 1996. Accessed August 4, 2015. http://www.historynet.com/railroads-critical-role-in-the-civil-war.htm.

McIntosh, Michael. *Best Guns*. Revised Edition. Camden, ME: Countrysport Press, 1999.

Murphy, David J. *Naval Strategy during the American Civil War*. Research Report. Montgomery, AL: Maxwell Air Force Base, 1999. Accessed August 17, 2015. http://www.dtic.mil/dtic/tr/fulltext/u2/a395177.pdf.

National Humanities Center. *The Triumph of Nationalism: The Nation Dividing*. Accessed July 21, 2015. http://nationalhumanitiescenter.org/pds/triumphnationalism/timeline.pdf.

National Park Service. "The Pratt Street Riot." Fort McHenry. Accessed August 4, 2015. http://www.nps.gov/fomc/learn/historyculture/the-pratt-street-riot.htm.

Peck, Michael. "The 5 Deadliest US Weapons of War from World War II." *National Interest*, January 25, 2015. Accessed August 22, 2015. http://nationalinterest.org/feature/the-5-deadliest-us-weapons-war-world-war-ii-12105.

Signal Corps Association. "Weaponry of 1860–1865 Corps." Accessed August 8, 2015. http://www.civilwarsignals.org/pages/signal/signalpages/weapons.html.

Simpson, James. "Steam Trains Were 19th-century Super Weapons." *War Is Boring*. Accessed August 3, 2015. https://medium.com/war-is-boring/steam-trains-were-19th-century-super-weapons-f4899564ee6d.

Sofge, Erik. "Top 5 High-Tech Guns for the Next-Gen Infantry." *Popular Mechanics*, July 13, 2008. Accessed August 14, 2015. http://www.popularmechanics.com/military/weapons/a3425/4273222.

Stacey, Robert. "American Wars to 1860." In *Military Communications from Ancient Times to the 21st Century*, edited by Christopher H. Sterling, 23–24. Santa Barbara, CA: ABC-CLIO, Inc., 2008.

Thulesius, Olav. "U.S.S. Monitor: A Cheesebox on a Raft." *America's Civil War*, November 2006. Accessed August 10, 2015. http://www.civilwar.org/battlefields/hampton-roads/hampton-roads-history/uss-monitor-a-cheesebox-on-a.html.

Towsley, Bryce. "Remington 2020 Sighting System." *American Rifleman*, December 17, 2013. Accessed August 21, 2015. http://www.americanrifleman.org/articles/2013/12/17/remington-2020-sighting-system.

Transportation Research Board. *This is Light Rail Transit*. November 2000. Accessed August 13, 2015. http://www.apta.com/resources/reportsandpublications/Documents/light_rail_bro.pdf.

US Army Transportation Museum. *The American Revolutionary War*. Accessed August 1, 2015. http://www.transchool.lee.army.mil/museum/transportation%20museum/revolutionary.htm.

FURTHER INFORMATION

Websites

American Rails

www.american-rails.com

Created and maintained by an individual with a passion for railroads, this site has a wealth of general and detailed information on the history, development, and current status of railroads in America.

Civil War Trust

www.civilwar.org

Created to preserve the Civil War battlegrounds, this nonprofit organization provides printed and online lessons, articles, primary documents, maps, photos, and other resources on every aspect of the Civil War.

US History: Pre-Columbian to the New Millennium

www.ushistory.org/us

Produced by the Independence Hall Association in Philadelphia, this easy-to-navigate website provides a comprehensive history of America. For each topic covered, the website has numerous links to primary source material and interesting sidebar-type information.

Video

US Civil War Weapons and Tactics: Civil War Technology – Military Documentary Film

www.youtube.com/watch?v=hOw_LJbLHlw

This forty-five-minute video depicts many of the military technologies of the Civil War and shows their relation to modern weapons and tactics.

INDEX

Page numbers in **boldface** are illustrations. Entries in **boldface** are glossary terms.

abolitionist, 13, 16, 22, **23**
Amtrak, 91, **92**
antebellum, 6, 10, 15, 19

ballistics, 96–97
battles
  Bull Run (Manassas), **4**, 47, 51
  Chattanooga, 51–52
  Hampton Roads, **71**, 72–73
  Mobile Bay, **64**
  Petersburg, **45**, 85
Beauregard, P. G. T., 27, 47, 51
Bleeding Kansas, 22–23
blockade, **40**, 41, 47, 66–69, 72–73, **85**, 86
bore, 37, 56, 96
Brown, John, **23**
brown navy, 73
Burton, James, 57–58

Calhoun, John C., 15
caliber, 37
carbine, **83**, 84
Carnegie, Andrew, 48–49, **48**
casemate, 69, 72
Clay, Henry, **14**, 20–21
Compromise of 1850, **14**, 21
Congress, **14**, 17, 19–22, 69, 81, 91
cotton, 7, 8, **9**, 10, 15–16, 22, 46
Crimean War, 57, 67
Cumberland Road, 11

Davis, Jefferson, 26, 58, 82
Deep South, 16, 25
Douglas, Stephen, 21–22

Ericsson, John, 69–70, 73
Erie Canal, 11, **12**

Fort Sumter, **26**, 27, 36, 65–66
Free State, 16–17, 19, 21–25, 78
frigate, 68, 72
Fugitive Slave Act, 21, 26
Fulton, Robert, 66

Gatling gun, 80, 84–85
Greener, William, 59

Hunley (Confederate submarine), 87, 99

Industrial Revolution, 7, 10–11, 13, 29, 43, 66, 75–76
ironclads, **41**, **64**, 67–73, **71**, 76, 86, 89–90, 98–99

Kansas-Nebraska Act, 22

Lee, Robert E., **23**, 78
Lincoln, Abraham, 24–27, 36, 40, 49, 53, 66, 70, **74**
logistics, 44, 66, 76
Louisiana Purchase, 6, 16, 19

Manassas, CSS, 67–69
manifest destiny, 6, 78
Merrimack, 68–69
    See also *Virginia*, CSS
Mexican War, 6, 21, 31, 33, 63
Minié, Claude-Étienne, 57, 59
minié bullet, 39–40, **54**, 55, 57–63, **62**, 76, 82, 85, 89–90, 93, 96
Missouri Compromise, 17, 19–20, 22
Monitor, USS, 69–73, **71**
Myer, Albert, 32

Napoleon III, 67
naval warfare
    after the Civil War, 98–99, **100–101**
    before the Civil War, 40, 66–67, 70
    during the Civil War, 40–41, **40**, **64**, 65–73, **71**, **85**, 86–87
Norton, John, 56–57

Pacific Railway Act, 81
Pratt Street Riot, 36

railhead, 77
Rail Passenger Service Act, 91
railroads
    after the Civil War, 80, **88**, 90–93, **92**, **94**, 95
    before the Civil War, 11–12, 22, 43–44
    during the Civil War, 35–36, **42**, 44–49, **45**, **50**, 51–53, 76–78
    standardization of, 46, 81
    transcontinental, 24, 78, **79**, 81, 91

reconnaissance, 62, 76
repeater, 39, 82, 84
Revolutionary War, 25, 30–31, 33, 35, **39**, 56, 82
rifling, 38, 56–59, 96–97

secede, 20, 25, 27, 65, 81
Second Great Awakening, 13
Sherman, William, **50**, 52, 77
Slater, Samuel, 7
slavery, 10, 13, 15–22, 24, 26
states' rights, 19–20, 24–26
steamships, 31, **40**, 41, 51, 66, 68–70, 73
strategy, 30–31, 53, 66, 73, 77, 82, 90
submarines, 41, 75, 87, 98–99

tactics, 38, 40, 44, 55, 60–63, 73, 76–77
Tariff of Abominations, 20
telegraph, 31–33, 43–44, 48–49, 53
torpedoes, 41, **85**, 86–87, 99

Union, 17–20, 25–27, 32, 36, **40**, **42**, 45, 47, 49, 51–53, 58, **60**, 65–69, 72–73, 78, **83**, 84, **85**, 86

Virginia, CSS, 69, 71–73, **71**

War of 1812, **26**, 31
weaponry
- after the Civil War, 93, 96–98, **97**
- before the Civil War, 35, 37–38, **39**, 55–58, 82, 84
- during the Civil War, 38–40, 55, 58, 60–63, 82, **83**, 84–85
- interchangeable parts and, 18

Whitney, Eli, 8, 18
wig wag, 32
Wilmot Proviso, 21
World War I, 75, **88**, 90
World War II, 90, 93

Zumwalt-class destroyer, 99, **100–101**

ABOUT THE AUTHOR

Born in Newport News, Virginia, just a few miles from where the ironclads fought, **Ann Byers** spent many of her childhood days at Hampton Roads, watching the ships of many countries go in and out of the harbor. Of the forty nonfiction books she has written on a variety of topics, her favorites are ones that tell the stories of great people and important events of the past. She has a degree in history and a particular passion for American history. In the summer of 2015, she and her husband spent several wonderful weeks exploring many of the battlefields of the Revolutionary and Civil Wars. Byers currently lives in California, where she is instilling a love of history in her eleven grandchildren.